Collins
easy learning
Spanish

in a click

Ronan Fitzsimons

HarperCollins Publishers
77-85 Fulham Palace Road
London W6 8JB
Great Britain

www.collinslanguage.com

First edition 2010

Reprint 10 9 8 7 6 5 4 3 2 1

© HarperCollins Publishers 2010

ISBN 978-0-00-733742-2

Collins® is a registered trademark of
HarperCollins Publishers Limited

A catalogue record for this book is available
from the British Library

Typeset by Q2AMedia

Audio material recorded and produced by
Networks SRL, Milan

Printed and Bound in China by Leo Paper
Products Ltd.

Editorial Director: Eva Martinez

Series Editor: Rob Scriven

Contents

Introduction

Welcome to *Collins Easy Learning Spanish in a Click*. This is a new course which aims to give you all the skills you'll need to start understanding and using Spanish quickly, easily and effectively in real situations.

This course is aimed at adult learners with no previous experience of Spanish. We've thought about which situations would be most useful to you during a visit to Spain, and have created a course that embraces all the main scenarios a traveller would be likely to encounter, such as public transport, checking into a hotel, shopping, eating out, visiting a museum and going to a football match.

Our approach is not to bombard you with too much grammar, but rather to let you listen to authentic dialogues set in useful situations, giving you the nuts and bolts of what's being said, then guiding you through carefully gauged practice exercises to increase your confidence.

The tools you need to succeed

The course has been designed to provide you with three essential tools in order to make your language learning experience a success. In your pack you'll find an activation code for the **online course**, this handy **book**, and an **audio CD**. You can use a combination of these whenever and wherever you are, making the course work for you.

The online course

www.collinslanguage.com/click provides you with a 12-unit online interactive language experience. Listen to a dialogue (and follow the words on-screen if you like) then study the new words and phrases before tackling some fun interactive games and exercises. You'll then also have the chance to perfect your pronunciation by recording your own voice (microphone not provided).

To access the online course simply go to www.collinslanguage.com/click and enter your personal activation code which you will find inside the front cover of this book.

The book

There will be times when it's not practical for you to be at a computer. There will also be times when you simply don't want to stare at the screen. For these times, this pocket-sized book contains the whole course for you in a handy portable format, so you can continue learning without the need for a computer. All of the content you need to learn Spanish is right here in this book. Study the language and complete the exercises just as you would online.

When you want to check your answers, go to **www.collinslanguage.com/click** to download the answer key.

The audio CD

Use the audio CD to hear native Spanish speakers engaging in dialogues set in real life situations and use it alongside the book in order to improve your listening comprehension skills. The audio CD can be downloaded to your mp3 player so that you can keep on learning even when you're on the move.

See the website at **www.collinslanguage.com/click** for the written transcript of all the spoken dialogues.

How it works

Spanish in a Click is divided into 12 units with revision sections after Unit 6 and Unit 12. Each unit begins with a **Traveller's tip**, a short passage highlighting an area of Spanish life and culture, offering you tips on what to expect when you visit the country.

Following a brief summary of the language structures you're about to study, we move straight on to the first dialogue, headed **Listen up**. Any tricky or useful vocabulary is then explained in the **Words and phrases** box (with accompanying audio online), then we go into a little more detail in **Unlocking the language**. Then it's over to you. **Your Turn** offers further practice of each structure and area of vocabulary encountered.

Halfway through each unit, you'll see that the cycle begins again with a fresh **Listen up**. This adds a different dimension to the material and scenario you've already looked at, and provides you with a new challenge in a slightly different situation.

Each unit ends with **Let's Recap**, in which you can check over the language you've used in the unit. The online version then gives you the chance to **record yourself** saying some of the most important vocabulary from the unit, to compare your pronunciation with that of a native speaker.

Collins Easy Learning Spanish in a Click aims to be fun, but at the same time to equip you with genuinely useful linguistic and cultural tools to make the most of your time in Spain. We hope you enjoy it! Good luck - *imucha suerte!*

6 seis

Mucho gusto
Pleased to meet you

We'll look at greetings and how to introduce yourself and say where you're from. You'll also learn how to say where you're going on holiday, and for how long.

Traveller's tip

The boom in affordable package holidays in the 1960s and 70s put Spain firmly on the map for foreign visitors, and its popularity continues to this day. There's more to Spain than **costas** and islands, though!

Recently, many people have started to travel to Spain independently, whether it be on a short city break, a whistle-stop tour of the major cities, or a fly -drive arrangement allowing them to spend a couple of weeks exploring the jewels of Andalucía in the south, the dramatic Picos de Europa in the north, or the ancient cities of Castilla in the centre. Pilgrims flock from all over the world to the Galician city of Santiago de Compostela in the north-west, and Valencia is starting to rival Madrid and Barcelona as a destination for tourists seeking spectacular culture and lively nightlife.

The rise of budget airlines, together with the drop in fares

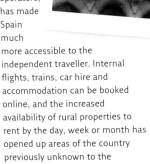

charged by long-distance operators, has made Spain much more accessible to the independent traveller. Internal flights, trains, car hire and accommodation can be booked online, and the increased availability of rural properties to rent by the day, week or month has opened up areas of the country previously unknown to the overseas tourist. You can find more details about this type of trip by searching for **agroturismo** or **turismo rural** on the internet.

Whatever type of visit to Spain you're planning, you'll quickly discover the truth of the old tourist-industry slogan **España: país de contrastes** - Spain, a country of contrasts.

In this unit we'll be working with two useful structures, to allow us to introduce ourselves and to say where we're going.

Soy ...   I am ...
Voy a ...   I'm going to ...

A British woman meets a Spanish man just before they catch a flight to Valencia. You can follow the conversation below as you listen to it, then you'll find a series of explanations and exercises linked to it on the next few pages.

Miguel	Hola.
Lynn	Hola, buenos días.
Miguel	¿Va usted a Valencia?
Lynn	Sí, voy a Valencia.
Miguel	Ah, yo también. Soy Miguel.
Lynn	Mucho gusto. Soy Lynn.
Miguel	¿Es usted inglesa?
Lynn	No, soy escocesa. Soy de Glasgow.
Miguel	Ah, usted es de Glasgow.
Lynn	¿Es usted de Valencia?
Miguel	No, soy de Bilbao, pero trabajo en Valencia. ¿Es usted estudiante?
Lynn	Sí, soy estudiante de español y francés.
Miguel	¿Va a Valencia a practicar el español?
Lynn	Sí, en un curso de verano.
Miguel	¡Muy bien! Bueno, voy a la cafetería.
Lynn	Vale. Hasta luego.
Miguel	Hasta luego.

Greetings, conventions, etc.

hola, buenos días	hello, good morning
sí, no	yes, no
yo también	so am I/me too
mucho gusto	pleased to meet you
pero	fine/very well
en un curso *m* de verano	on a summer course. **En** can mean both in or on.
muy bien	very good
bueno ...	well ...
vale	OK
hasta luego	see you later

Verbs

¿Va (usted) a ...?	Are you going to ...?
voy a ...	I'm going to ...
soy	I am
¿Es (usted) ...?	Are you ...?
trabajo	I work
practicar	to practise

Some nationalities

inglés/inglesa	English *m/f*
escocés/escocesa	Scottish *m/f*
español/española	Spanish *m/f*
francés/francesa	French *m/f*

A few jobs/occupations

estudiante	student
profesor/profesora	teacher *m/f*
artista	artist

In this section we explain some of the words and expressions introduced in the dialogue.

el español/**la** cafetería	'the Spanish language/the café'. To say 'the' in Spanish, we use the word **el** for a noun that is masculine, and **la** for feminine. All nouns in Spanish are considered either masculine or feminine.
¿Es usted inglesa/de Valencia/estudiante?	'**Are you** English/from Valencia/a student?' **Es** can also be used to mean 'it is': **es interesante** 'it's interesting'.
Soy escocesa/de Bilbao/ estudiante	'**I'm** Scottish/from Bilbao/a student'. **Soy** ('I am') and **es** ('you are') are both parts of the verb **ser** ('to be'). You can also see that 'I'm a student' is just **soy estudiante**. You don't say 'a' before a job or occupation in Spanish.
Soy estudiante de francés	I'm studying French - literally, this is 'I'm student of French'
ingl**és**/ingl**esa** españo**l**/españo**la**	Nationalities are spelt with a small letter, and that their endings vary depending on whether the person is male or female.
¿Va usted a Valencia? **Voy** a Valencia.	'**Are you going** to Valencia?' '**I'm going** to Valencia.' **Voy** ('I'm going') and **va** ('you're going') are both parts of the verb **ir** ('to go')

↗ Your turn 1

Listen again to the dialogue (track 1). Are the following statements 1 true or false? You will find the answers to all of the exercises in this book online at www.collinslanguage.com/click.

1. They are travelling to Barcelona. ....
2. Lynn is English. ....
3. Miguel works in Valencia. ....

- -

Check your understanding by answering these questions: ⊙ 1

1. What does Lynn study?
2. Where is Miguel going now?

Find expressions in the dialogue (track 1) to convey the following:

1. Good morning
2. pleased to meet you
3. me too
4. Are you going to Valencia?
5. Yes, I'm going to Valencia.
6. Are you a student?
7. Yes, I'm a student of French and Spanish.
8. see you later

Pronunciation Tip

Spanish pronunciation is generally straightforward, with each letter pronounced logically. Where there are difficulties, we'll give you guidance in the Pronunciation Tip section in each unit.

soy de Valencia

In Spanish the letters **b** and **v** are both pronounced as a gentle **b**.

español

The Spanish **ñ** is pronounced rather like the 'ni' in the English 'onion'. We'll do some more practice of this sound later.

. . . .

Ask a female the following questions. You can check your answers by listening to the audio track. 2

1. Are you French?
2. Are you English?

. . . .

Say the following in Spanish: 2

1. I am Spanish. (*Try both male and female forms.*)
2. I am from Valencia.
3. I am a student.

. . . .

Listen and see how much you can understand: 3

1. What is the man's name? . . . .
2. Where is he from? . . . .
3. What is Ana's nationality? . . . .
4. What is her job? . . . .

Match the Spanish expressions on the left with their meanings on the right. There are some new words – see if you can guess what they mean.

1.	Soy australiano/a.	Are you Irish?
2.	Trabajo en una oficina.	It's very interesting.
3.	Voy a la cafetería.	I study Italian.
4.	Soy estudiante de italiano.	I'm Australian.
5.	¿Es usted irlandés/irlandesa?	I'm going to the café.
6.	Es muy interesante.	I work in an office.

 ## Listen up 2

Listen to Álvaro and Beatriz talking about themselves, their work and their studies. Use the Words and Phrases and Unlocking the Language sections on the next page to help you understand the new language.

⊙ 4

Álvaro	Hola, buenas tardes. Soy Álvaro. Soy español, de Salamanca, pero vivo y trabajo en Barcelona. Soy ...profesor de matemáticas. También soy estudiante de fotografía. Ahora voy a clase de fotografía. Luego voy a un restaurante con los amigos de la clase.
Beatriz	Hola, soy Beatriz. Soy española, de Sevilla, pero vivo en Madrid. No trabajo. Soy estudiante de historia. Ahora voy a clase. Luego voy a un bar con mi novio.

Words and phrases 2

buenas tardes	good afternoon/evening. **Tarde** can also mean late.
vivo	I live
profesor/profesora de matemáticas	maths teacher *m/f*
fotografía *f*	photography

ahora	now
clase *f*	class
luego	later
con	with
restaurante	restaurant
no trabajo	I don't work
historia *f*	history
bar	bar
novio/novia	boyfriend/girlfriend

 ## Unlocking the language 2

viv**o** y trabaj**o**	'I live and (I) work'. Most verbs saying what I do ('I study', 'I travel', etc) end in –o in Spanish. Unfortunately, both **soy** and **voy** are exceptions!
un bar/**una** oficina	Notice that the word for 'a' can be **un** or **una**. This depends on whether the noun it goes with is considered masculine (**un bar**) or feminine (**una oficina**). **Un/una** can also mean 'one' – see below.
con los amigos de la clase/con mi novio	'with my classmates/with my boyfriend'.

Numbers 1–12

1	**uno** (when it stands alone) **un bar** – working with a masculine noun **una oficina** – working with a feminine noun
2, 3, 4, 5, 6, 7	**dos, tres, cuatro, cinco, seis, siete**
8, 9, 10, 11, 12	**ocho, nueve, diez, once, doce**

Fill in the gaps to check you understood the descriptions on track 4:

1.   Hola, buenas tardes. .... Alvaro. Soy ...., de

Salamanca, pero vivo y trabajo en .... Soy profesor de matemáticas.

También soy .... de fotografía. Ahora .... a clase de

fotografía. Luego......................... a un restaurante con los amigos de la ....

2.   ...., soy Beatriz. Soy ...., de Sevilla, pero vivo en

.... No trabajo. .... estudiante de historia. Ahora

.... a clase. Luego .... a un bar con mi novio.

· ·

Rewrite the following to create Spanish numbers:

CHOO	ROTCAU	SERT	VEUNE	CONE
....	....	....	....	....

ZIDE	EISS	AUN	ODS	NICCO
....	....	....	....	....

NU	TIESE	NOU	CODE	
....	....	....	....	

· ·

Say the following in Spanish. Check your answers by listening to
the audio track.   5

1.   Hello

2.   I am English. *(try both male and female)*

3.   I live in Barcelona.

4.   I am a student.

Listen and understand. In which order are the numbers 1–12 pronounced? Mark the order against the list of Spanish numbers below: 6

uno	cuatro	siete	diez ....
dos	cinco	ocho	once ....
tres	seis	nueve	doce ....

· ·

There are two mistakes in the following text. Can you spot them?

Hola, buenos días. Soy María. Soy español. Vivo en Málaga pero soy Madrid. Soy economista.

Let's recap

Here's an opportunity for you to revise the language you've learned in this unit.

Supply the correct option in each case.

1. ¿ .... usted española?

   a. Soy   **b.** Va   **c.** Es

2. No, no .... española.

   a. va   **b.** soy   **c.** voy

3. ¿ .... usted a Valencia?

   a. Voy   **b.** Es   **c.** Va

4. Sí, ... a Valencia.

   a. es   **b.** voy   **c.** soy

· ·

Write the numbers 1–12 in Spanish. We've started you off:

1. uno	7. ....
2. dos	8. ....
3.	9. ....
4.	10. ....
5.	11. ....
6.	12. ....

¿Dónde está ...?
Where is ...?

You'll learn how to find your way around using public transport, and to locate places you need to find. We'll also study how to say what time things happen.

Traveller's tip

Public transport in Spain is efficient and excellent value for money. Local bus services - and, in some of the larger cities, tram and **metro** (underground train) networks - have benefited from huge investment and visitors are often surprised at how cheap transport is when compared with their home countries.

One of the main advantages of the bus system in Spanish cities is that there is generally one (very reasonable) fixed fare, however many stops you wish to travel. A single ticket will usually allow you to combine travel on a bus and a metro train to reach your destination. Further savings can be made by buying a multi-journey ticket - **un billete multiviaje** - giving you, say, ten journeys for the price of eight.

Travelling between cities by train is a delight in modern, clean, comfortable trains which are also remarkably affordable. The national rail network, **RENFE**, has a number of inter-city jewels in its crown, notably the high-speed **AVE** between Madrid and Barcelona and the **Euromed**, linking the cities of the east coast.

If you're on a limited budget, a wealth of privately-run coach companies offer services criss-crossing the country as well as stretching into Portugal, France and beyond.

Iberia Airways offers a surprisingly affordable shuttle service known as the **Puente Aéreo** - literally 'air bridge' - between Madrid and Barcelona. The journey takes less than an hour, and is enjoyed by a mixture of business travellers heading for meetings, and tourists keen to have breakfast in one city and lunch in the other!

In the last unit we met a verb for 'to be' – **ser** – which we used to say things about ourselves. Now we're going to use the other verb 'to be' – **estar** – which is used to say where things are located. We'll also learn the language you need to say what time a bus or train leaves and arrives.

¿A qué hora ...?   At what time ...?
¿Dónde está ...?   Where is ...?

 Listen up 1

We've arrived in Spain and are outside the airport looking to continue our journey to our destination. Listen to this sequence of short dialogues as many times as you need to.   ⊙ 7

First we need to ask where the bus stop is:

Tourist	Hola.
Passer-by	Buenos días.
Tourist	¿Dónde está la parada de autobús?
Passer-by	Está allí, a la derecha.
Tourist	Ah, sí. Gracias.
Passer-by	De nada.

Now we're in the city centre looking for the underground station.   ⊙ 8
Another passer-by is telling us that it's in the main street:

Tourist	Por favor, ¿dónde está la estación de metro?
Passer-by	Está en la calle principal.
Tourist	Muchas gracias.
Passer-by	De nada.

Now we need to buy a ticket – just a one-way ticket for the first   ⊙ 9
journey. You'll hear the expression for 'one-way', as well as the price:

Tourist	Un billete de ida, por favor.
Clerk	Dos euros.
Tourist	Gracias.

Now we're going on a day trip to the historic Catalan town of
Tarragona, but this time we need a return ticket. Listen carefully
and try and catch the price:

Tourist	Voy a Tarragona, ida y vuelta. ¿Cuánto es?
Clerk	Son doce euros, por favor.
Tourist	Muchas gracias.
Clerk	De nada. Hasta luego.
Tourist	Adiós.

🔊 Words and phrases 1

¿Dónde está ...?	Where is ...?
Está ...	It's ...
la parada de autobús	the bus stop
allí/aquí	there/here
a la derecha / a la izquierda	on the right / on the left
gracias	thank you. You may also hear **muchas gracias** - thank you very much.
de nada	you're welcome/not at all
por favor	please
la estación de metro	the underground station
la calle principal	the main street
un billete de ida	a single ticket
(un billete de) ida y vuelta	(a) return (ticket)
¿Cuánto es?	How much is (it)?
hasta luego	see you later (lit. until later)
adiós	goodbye

One of the potentially confusing things about Spanish is that there are two ways of saying 'to be'. We learned about **ser** in Unit 1. The other verb, **estar**, is used to talk about where something is - where it's located:

¿Dónde **está** la parada?   Where's the stop?

Está allí/**Está** en   It's there/It's in/on

Ser is used for many purposes: we've already seen **soy Miguel**, **soy español**, **soy de Madrid**, **soy economista**, and now we can add prices to this list:

¿Cuánto **es** (el billete)?   How much is it (is the ticket)?

Es un euro/**son** dos euros.   It's one euro/two euros.

Notice that for something costing two euros upwards, the seller will say **son** (lit. 'they are', rather than 'it is').

You may have noticed the Spanish convention of putting an inverted question mark ¿ at the start of a question. The same happens with a ¡ at the start of an exclamation.

You'll also have noticed the accent on the word **está**. The rules for why a word has an accent are quite complicated, but a useful guide is that you should pronounce any vowel with an accent on it more heavily than other vowels in the word: e.g. **ess-TAH**, whereas without the accent, **esta** would be **ESS-tah**.

 Your turn 1

True or false? Remember that you can check your answers online at www.collinslanguage.com/click.   ◉ 9-10

1.   The single ticket was 3 euros. . . . .

2.   The return to Tarragona was 12 euros. . . . .

· ·

Match the photos with the Spanish word for each form of transport:

1.   el autobús

2.   el metro

3.   el taxi

4.   el tren

a.

b.

c.

d.

Find expressions in the dialogues to convey the following: 7-10

1. Where is the bus stop?
2. Where is the metro station?
3. How much is it?
4. It's twelve euros.

. . . .

Make sure you can also say the following:

1. hello
2. please
3. thanks
4. many thanks
5. you're welcome/not at all
6. goodbye

Pronunciation Tip

en la calle principal
You can choose one of two ways to pronounce the Spanish 'll':

Like the English 'y' as in 'yacht' – **calle** *ka-yeh*

Or like the 'lli' in the English 'million' – **calle** *kal-yeh*

Try them both and see which one you're more comfortable with,
then try the word **billete** (a ticket) a few times.

. . . .

Ask for the following tickets in Spanish. Check your answers by listening to the audio track. 11

1. To Barcelona, return, please.
2. A single ticket

Now try and remember how to ask these two questions. Again, ⊙ 12
listen to the audio track to check your answers.

1. Where is the bus stop? ....

2. How much is it? ....

· ·

Listen to the conversation on track 13 and then answer the ⊙ 13
following questions:

1. Where does the woman want to go? ....

2. What sort of ticket does she ask for? ....

3. How much does it cost? ....

· ·

Rearrange the word order in these expressions so that they make sense:

1. favor ida por de un billete ....

2. ¿estación está dónde la? ....

3. euros diez son ....

4. principal la en calle está ....

Listen up 2

Making enquiries at the bus station. The passenger wants to get a ⊙ 14
bus to the capital. He's told what time it leaves and what time it
arrives. Listen out for the patterns of how times are expressed:

Passenger	¿A qué hora sale el autobús?
Clerk	Sale a las cuatro y media.
Passenger	Y ¿a qué hora llega a Madrid?
Clerk	Llega a las seis menos cuarto, aproximadamente.
Passenger	Muchas gracias.

Now we're at the railway station. The customer wants to go to
the university town of Salamanca. This time, you'll hear not only
the departure and arrival times, but also the price of the ticket:

⊙ 15

Customer	Buenas tardes.
Clerk	Hola, buenas tardes.
Customer	¿A qué hora sale el tren para Salamanca?
Clerk	Sale a las diez.
Customer	Y ¿a qué hora llega a Salamanca?
Clerk	Llega a Salamanca a las once y cinco.
Customer	¿Cuánto es?
Clerk	Son seis euros ida sólo, y once euros ida y vuelta.
Customer	Muy bien. Gracias.
Clerk	De nada.

❛❜ Words and phrases 2

¿A qué hora sale?	(At) What time does it leave?
autobus *m*	bus
Sale ...	It leaves/departs ...
y	and
¿A qué hora llega?	(At) What time does it arrive?
Llega ...	It arrives ...
aproximadamente	approximately
tren *m*	train
ida sólo	just one way

🔓 Unlocking the language 2

Telling the time

¿a qué hora?	The basic question really asks 'at what hour?' You have already met the word **a** in a situation where it meant 'to' (**Voy a Valencia** 'I'm going to Valencia'). Here, instead, it means 'at'. Then you can add a verb:
¿A qué hora **llega**?	'At what time **does it arrive**?'
Llega a las once.	**It arrives** at eleven o'clock. Notice that the verb is the same in the question and the answer.

veintitrés 23

'At' a particular time

a la una	at one o'clock
a las dos	at two o'clock
a las tres	at three o'clock

Notice that the **la** at 1.00 becomes **las** for times from 2.00 to 12.00.

Here's how to say some more complex times:

at 11.05	a las once **y** cinco		at 11.45	a las doce **menos** cuarto
at 11.10	a las once **y** diez		at 11.50	a las doce **menos** diez
at 11.15	a las once **y cuarto**		at 11.55	a las doce **menos** cinco
at 11.30	a las once **y media**			

So **y** matches the 'past' half of the English clock, and **menos** equates to minutes 'to' the next hour.

Two more useful words: **mediodía** 'midday' and **medianoche** 'midnight'.

Match up the clock faces with the times shown beneath:

1. las cinco y cuarto
2. las siete menos cuarto
3. las once y diez
4. las nueve

a.

b.

c.

d.

. . . .

Write the following in full in Spanish:

1. at 4.10 ....

2. at 6.15 ....

3. at 9.30 ....

4. at 10.45 ....

5. at 12.55 *(be careful!)* ....

Can you say the following in Spanish? Check your answers by listening to the audio track. ⊙ 16

1. The train leaves at three o'clock.   2. The bus arrives at ten o'clock.

Listen to the conversation and try to answer these three questions: ⊙ 17

1. Where is the passenger going? ....

2. What time does the train leave? ....

3. What time does it get to its destination? ....

Answer the following questions in Spanish using the prompts in brackets:

1. ¿Dónde está la estación de metro? (*main street*)

2. ¿Cuánto es un billete de ida? (*4 euros*)

3. ¿A qué hora sale el tren? (*9.15*)

4. ¿A qué hora llega el autobús? (*9.50*)

🔄 Let's recap

Use one of the following words to fill each of the gaps below:

sale	el	a	llega	a	está
cuánto	cuarto	billete	dónde	hora	

1. ¿.................... .... la parada de autobús?

2. ¿.................... qué hora .... el tren para Madrid?

3. Sale a las dos menos ....

4. ¿A qué hora .... a Madrid?

5. ¿A qué .... sale ......,............ autobús?

6. ¿.................... es un .... de ida y vuelta?

7. Está .... la derecha.

Un poco de ayuda
A bit of help

3

We'll put together an essential survival kit, to cover any situations in which you might run into problems, from simply not understanding to more complex situations such as health issues and loss of possessions.

Traveller's tip

Among the problems expressed by students of Spanish are the notions that Spaniards talk much more quickly than speakers of English, and that regional accents can be hard to follow. It's a fact that accents from the south of the country tend to be more difficult to understand, as various letters and word-endings seem to be missed off. The speed issue may or may not be true, but it's inevitable that there will be times when you don't catch what's been said to you, so we're going to focus on a few expressions to make it clear that you haven't understood, to ask for repetitions, and so on.

You may find you've simply taken a wrong turning and can't find your way back to the hotel, or to the particular square or museum you're looking for. It's a good idea to have the basics of asking for (and understanding) directions from A to B.

It's fair to say that Spain is generally a safe, friendly and easy-going place to spend time, but in any city or country there will always be the minority element looking to pick your pocket or trick you in some way. We'll show you what you need to say if you've lost your passport, money, etc.

Equally, there's no legislating for when accidents or illnesses can strike, at home or abroad. We'll equip you with the basic language necessary to explain what's happened so that you can get the correct treatment.

In this unit, as well as focusing on situation-specific language, we'll dip briefly into the past tense to say what has happened. This is a one-off – the rest of the course returns to primarily present-tense language.

| **He perdido mi pasaporte.** | I've lost my passport. |
| **Me han robado la cartera.** | I've had my wallet stolen. |

We'll also have a look at the verb **poder** ('to be able') to ask questions like 'Can you help me?'

| **¿Me puede ayudar?** | Can you help me? |

 ## Listen up 1

Listen to the series of short expressions on the audio track covering problems of understanding. You'll have the opportunity to practise them shortly.

◎ 18

What if you get lost? Listen to this next set of useful expressions. Again, explanations and exercises will follow.

◎ 19

From now on the dialogues will not be shown in this book. If you still feel you would like to see them you can always download them from www.collinslangiage.com/click.

Words and phrases 1

¿Cómo?	Pardon?
¿Puede repetir, por favor?	Can you repeat that, please?
más despacio	more slowly
No entiendo.	I don't understand.
No hablo español.	I don't speak Spanish.
¿Habla usted inglés?	Do you speak English?
Soy extranjero/a.	I'm a foreigner. *m/f*
No soy de aquí.	I'm not from here.
¿Me lo apunta, por favor?	Can you write it down for me, please?

perdón/perdone	sorry (excuse me) – **perdone** is a slightly more formal way of excusing yourself
¿Me puede ayudar?	Can you help me?
¡Socorro!	Help!
estoy perdido/a	I'm lost *m/f*
¿Dónde está la plaza mayor?	Where's the main square?
¿Dónde está el Hotel Central?	Where's the Hotel Central?
¿Dónde está el baño?	Where's the toilet?
¿Para ir a la estación de trenes?	Which way to the railway station?
¿Me indica en el plano dónde estoy?	Can you show me on the map where I am?

🔓 Unlocking the language 1

no entiendo no hablo español no soy de aquí	Notice that in order to make any verb negative, you just put **no** before it. **Entiendo** means 'I understand'; **No entiendo** means 'I don't understand'.
¿Me puede ayudar? ¿Puede repetir?	**Puede** ('you can' or 'can you?') is part of the verb **poder** ('to be able') and is very useful for asking if someone **can** do something. For the verb that follows it, such as 'help' or 'repeat', just use the infinitive form (the word as you find it in the dictionary) – you don't need to do any work to it!
perdón	'Excuse me/sorry.' As well as the general **perdón**, here are some other ways of saying sorry that can be used both for attracting attention and for apologising: **Perdona** (*informal*)/**perdone** (*polite*) **Disculpa** (*informal*)/**disculpe** (*polite*) You can also use **oye** (*informal*)/**oiga** (*polite*) to attract attention while **lo siento** is used purely for apologising.
¿Para ir a ...?	Literally meaning 'For going to ...?', this is used to mean 'To get to ...?'
¿Dónde está ...? Está ...	'Where is ...?' 'It's (located) ...' When dealing with something's location or position, remember that Spanish uses the verb **estar** to convey the 'is' or 'it is' part of the sentence.
dónde?/donde	This isn't important when you're speaking, of course, but we can note in passing that the question word for 'where?' carries a written accent in Spanish, to distinguish it from 'where' in a non-questioning sense like 'the house where I live'. This is not uncommon in Spanish.

Spend a few minutes re-reading Words and phrases 1, then see if you can remember expressions to convey the following. Remember that you can check your answers by going online to www.collinslanguage.com/click.

1. I don't understand.

2. Can you repeat, please?

3. more slowly

4. I'm not from here.

5. Can you write it down for me, please?

6. Can you help me?

The Spanish alphabet

◉ 20

a	(ah)	**ñ**	(enn-yeh)
b	(beh)	**o**	(oh)
c	(like 'the' in English 'theft')	**p**	(peh)
ch	(as in 'Che' Guevara)	**q**	(kuu)
d	(like 'de' in English 'deaf')	**r**	(erre, a bit like the English 'air raid')
e	(eh)		
f	(like first 4 letters of English 'effect')	**s**	(ess-eh)
g	(guttural 'he' of English 'help')	**t**	(teh)
h	(at-che)	**u**	(oo, as in 'food')
i	(ee, like the beginning of the English 'even')	**v**	(oo-veh)
j	(guttural hoh-tah)	**w**	(oo-veh-dob-leh)
k	(kah)	**x**	(ek-eess)
l	(ell-eh)	**y**	(ee-gree-ehh-gah, literally 'Greek letter i')
ll	(el-yeh)		
m	(emm-eh)	**z**	(theta, like 'the' in English 'theft', plus 'tah')
n	(enn-eh)		

It would be useful at this point to study carefully the letters needed to spell your name and the street and town where you live. Practise spelling these out until you can do it without looking at the guide.

Pronunciation Tip

me puede ayudar/¿me puede ayudar?

As we mentioned earlier on, there's no difference in the written form of a statement and a question, except for the question marks. However, in the spoken form, the question will tend to raise its pitch at the end, just as it would in English. Try saying the expression on the left a few times, first as a statement ('you can help me') then as a question ('can you help me?')

. . . .

How would you say the following in Spanish? Check your answers by listening to the audio track. 21

1. I'm lost (*spoken by a man*)

2. I'm lost (*spoken by a woman*)

3. I'm foreign (*spoken by a man*)

4. I'm foreign (*spoken by a woman*)

. . . .

Listen to the people talking, and make sure you have understood the problems they're describing: 22

1. Where does the first person want to go?

2. Where is the second speaker from?

. . . .

Match the predicaments on the left with the English translations on the right:

1. Para ir a ...?   I'm a foreigner

2. Soy extranjero/a   I'm lost

3. No entiendo   I don't speak Spanish

4. Estoy perdido/a   To go to ...?

5. No hablo español   I don't understand

Listen up 2

En la comisaría de policía/At the police station
@ 23

Listen to the dialogue between a tourist and a police officer. The explanatory sections will help with any words you can't pick out first time.

En el hospital (Urgencias)/At the hospital (Accident and Emergency)
@ 24

Now listen to a tourist explaining his health condition at the A & E reception desk.

Remember that all of the dialogues are available in written form online at www.collinslanguage.com/click.

Words and phrases 2

¿Qué le pasa?	What's the problem? (lit. 'What happens to you?')
Me han robado la cartera.	I've had my wallet stolen.
¿Cuándo?	When?
esta mañana	this morning. **Mañana** also means tomorrow.
¿No ha visto a nadie?	You didn't see anyone?
he perdido	I've lost
pasaporte *m*	passport
dinero *m*	money
llave *f*	key
no se preocupe	don't worry (polite form)
vamos a llamar	let's call (lit. we're going to call)
hotel *m*	hotel
consulado *m*	consulate
no hay de qué	not at all – an alternative to **de nada**
rellene este formulario	fill out this form
nombre *m*	first name
apellido *m*	surname
domicilio *m*	home address

nacionalidad *f*	nationality
Tengo el brazo hinchado.	my arm is swollen (lit. 'I have the arm swollen')
¿Le duele? Me duele.	Does it hurt (you)?/It hurts (me). Add **mucho** to mean 'a lot': **me duele mucho**.
médico *m/f*	doctor
¿Cuál es su nombre?	What's your name?
canadiense	Canadian
estar de vacaciones	to be on holiday
tarjeta *f* de seguro médico	Health insurance card. **Tarjeta** means card. You will also hear it used in the phrase **tarjeta de crédito** - credit card. If you are an EU citizen, get hold of a European Health Insurance Card: it entitles you to the same treatment as Spanish residents.
siéntese un momento	Have a seat for a moment
móvil *m*	mobile phone

 ## Unlocking the language 2

Me han robado ...	'I've had my ... stolen.' Don't worry about the complicated structure: just learn **me han robado** (+ name of item) as a one-off.
He perdido ...	This is another past tense – again, just focus on the meaning rather than how it's formed. You can start your explanation with **he perdido** ..., then list any items lost.
mi pasaporte	'my passport'. **Mi** means 'my'. If you want to say 'your' use **su**: **¿Cuál es su nombre?** 'What is your name?'
¿Me da ...?	'Will you give me ...?/May I have ...?' This is an example of where Spanish speakers are very direct; this is perfectly polite, unlike in English where directness can sometimes seem rude.
rellene	**Rellenar** is the verb 'to complete/fill out (a form)'.
¿le duele (el brazo)? me duele (el brazo)	**Duele** comes from **doler** ('to hurt'). What is being said here is 'does it hurt you?'/'it hurts me'. If it's needed, the suffering body part comes after the **duele** in both question and statement. **Me duele mucho** means it hurts a lot.

Match the following photos with the Spanish words next to them:

1. las llaves
2. el dinero
3. la tarjeta de crédito
4. el móvil
5. el pasaporte
6. la cartera

a.

b.

c.

d.

e.

f.

Find expressions in the dialogues (tracks 23 & 24) to convey the following: 23-24

1. Can you help me, please?
2. I've had my wallet stolen.
3. I've lost my passport.
4. My arm is swollen.
5. It hurts.

Can you say the following in Spanish? The language that you know ⦿ 25
from the dialogue has been rearranged slightly. Check your answers
by listening to the audio track.

1. I've had my passport stolen.
2. I've lost my wallet.
3. This morning at ten o'clock.

Listen to these two people telling you what has happened to them 26
and then answer the questions?

1. What has been lost in the first instance? ....
2. What's the problem in the second situation? ....

Here are some other body parts that might be hurting you. See if you
can match them up: we haven't learned them yet, so you'll need to guess!
Or you could use the free dictionary at www.collinslanguage.com.

1. ... la cabeza   my tooth

2. ... la muela   my stomach

3. ... el pie   my head

4. ... el estómago   my leg

5. ... la pierna   my foot

Let's recap

In this unit we've set out a couple of usages of a past tense. There's no
need to learn the tense, but the expressions themselves are handy to keep
in mind. Here's a reminder:

Me han robado ...   I've had my ... stolen

He perdido ...   I've lost ...

· ·

The following sentences have their words in the wrong order. Can you
rectify them?

1. ¿favor ayudar puede por me? ....

2. ¿dónde indica el estoy plano en me? ....

3. cartera me robado la han ....

4. brazo me mucho el duele ....

· ·

Choose the correct option to complete each sentence:

1. ¿Me da .... pasaporte?

    a. de   **b.** la   **c.** su   **d.** una

2. ¿Dónde .... el Hotel Central?

    a. es   **b.** soy   **c.** estoy   **d.** está

3. Rellene .... formulario.

    a. esta   **b.** este   **c.** estas   **d.** estos

4. ¿Le .... mucho?

    a. brazo   **b.** duele   **c.** hay   **d.** problema

En el hotel
At the hotel

4

We'll cover the language you'll need to check into a hotel in Spain and discover what facilities it has to offer. We'll also be taking a look at some of the different types of places to stay in Spain.

Traveller's tip

Every year, millions of us head to Spain seeking sunshine, good food and drink, culture and relaxation.

Most hotel and tourism staff speak some English. However, there's a real achievement in speaking some Spanish on holiday, and Spaniards will be delighted you've made an effort to learn their language.

Our first experience of a Spanish hotel is usually on the coasts or islands as part of a package holiday. But next time, you may want to do things more independently. Here are some of the key words in considering accommodation.

On a modest budget, **una pensión** or **un hostal** could be for you – modest establishments, often family-run, sometimes with breakfast and private bathroom, but generally without. Facilities are basic, and credit cards are often not accepted.

Backpackers should look out for **un albergue**, a (youth) hostel. Expect a multicultural environment and a lively time, for a very reasonable price.

Un hotel is indeed a hotel. Expect a higher level of service (and price!), usually with en-suite facilities, air-conditioning, etc. Credit cards are widely accepted, and most Spanish hotels take bookings online.

For an atmospheric, historical setting, try **un parador**. These are a chain of state-run hotels, luxuriously appointed but surprisingly affordable. They have invariably been converted from monasteries, convents, castles, stately homes or former municipal buildings. Check out the website: **www.parador.es**.

In this unit, we'll mainly be revising two structures we met earlier. They're both very useful for finding your way around and planning your time.

| **¿Dónde están ...?** | Where are ...? (Notice that this time, we're asking about plural things – see below for examples.) |
| **¿A qué hora es ...?** | At what time is ...? |

 Listen up 1

A couple arrive at a Spanish hotel and check in. Listen to the dialogue and see if you can pick out the various stages of the process.

◉ 27

Remember that you can see all of the dialogues in written form by going online to www.collinslanguage.com/click.

Words and phrases 1

somos		we are
Tenemos una habitación reservada.		We have a room booked.
señor/señora		Mr/Mrs
habitación *f*		bedroom
una habitación	individual	a single room
	doble	a double room
	con cama de matrimonio	with a double bed
	con dos camas	with two beds (i.e. a twin room)

	con baño	with an en-suite bathroom
	con ducha	with a shower
noche *f*		night
tienen		you have/they have
planta *f* – en la cuarta planta, en la primera planta		storey/floor – on the fourth floor, on the first floor
ascensor *m*		lift
desayuno *m*/desayunar		breakfast/to have breakfast
cena *f*/cenar		dinner/to have an evening meal
vamos de tapas		we're going out for a few tapas
necesita		you need
algo más		something else/anything else

🔓 Unlocking the language 1

para diez noches	'for ten nights'. When you're booking something 'for' a period of time, remember to use **para** + (**dos horas, tres días, siete noches**, etc.)
aquí tiene	'here you are'. This is the response to **¿Me da ...?** in the dialogue.
Está a la izquierda/ a la derecha.	'It's on the left/right.'
todo recto	'straight ahead' – another handy phrase that you may not need to use yourself but you might hear others say to you.
primero, segundo, tercero	'first, second, third'. The word for 'fourth' is **cuarto** (the same as for 'quarter'), 'fifth' is **quinto**. If they are being used with a feminine word like **planta**, they become feminine too: **primera, segunda** ...

Numbers 13–29

In unit 1, we looked at numbers from 1 to 12. Here's the next batch, from 13 to 29. Notice that each of them is just a single word:

13 trece
14 catorce
15 quince

Notice the structure of the next few: e.g. 18 is composed of 'ten and eight'.

16 dieciséis
17 diecisiete
18 dieciocho
19 diecinueve
20 veinte

From 21 to 29, you'll see a structure of 'twenty and one', 'twenty and two', and so on:

21 veintiuno
22 veintidós
23 veintitrés
24 veinticuatro
25 veinticinco
26 veintiséis
27 veintisiete
28 veintiocho
29 veintinueve

Numbers 30–99

Now let's look at higher numbers from 30 to 99. Note that in this range, the number will always be composed of three words, unless it's a multiple of ten, like 30, 40 and so on. The format is the multiple of ten + **y** ('and') + the corresponding single digit.

30 treinta
31 treinta y uno
32 treinta y dos
40 cuarenta
46 cuarenta y seis
50 cincuenta
60 sesenta
70 setenta
80 ochenta
90 noventa
99 noventa y nueve

Be careful with the similarity between 60 and 70.

Check your understanding of the dialogue by answering these
questions. Remember to check you answers online afterwards:
www.collinslanguage.com/click.   ◉ 27

1. How many nights will they be staying? ....

2. What is the room number? ....

3. What time is breakfast? ....

4. What time is dinner? ....

• •

Find expressions in the dialogue to convey the following: ◉ 27

1. We have a room booked.

2. for ten nights

3. your passport and your
    credit card

4. on the first floor

5. Dinner is at nine o'clock
    in the evening.

6. Is there anything else
    you need?

7. see you later

Pronunciation Tip

una cita para cenar (a dinner date)

The combination **ce** is pronounced like the
beginning of the English word 'theft'. Similarly,
ci is pronounced like the beginning of the
English 'thief'.

Try some more:

Habitación dieciséis (room 16)

¿Necesita algo más? (Do you need anything
else?)

• •

Now, using the language you've learned above, think about arriving   ◉ 28
at a hotel, but this time with slightly different requirements. How
would you say the following? Check your answers by listening to the
audio track.

1. A single room with a shower.

2. A double room with an en-suite
    bathroom.

3. A twin room.

4. A room with a double bed.

5. A room for fourteen nights.

Listen to the guests and make sure you have understood their 29
requirements:

1. What sort of room does the first man mention? ....
2. How many nights will the woman be staying? ....
3. What bathroom facility does the man specify? ....

• •

Match the questions on the left with the answers on the right:

1.	¿Me da su pasaporte, por favor?	Es a las ocho.
2.	¿Dónde está el ascensor?	No, gracias.
3.	¿A qué hora es el desayuno?	Está aquí a la izquierda.
4.	¿Necesita algo?	Sí, aquí tiene.

Listen up 2

Later the same day, Claire wants to find a
good local tapas bar, so she returns to the
hotel reception desk for advice. Listen to
the dialogue (and follow it online if you like).

30

Words and phrases 2

pregunta *f*	question
hoy	today
cenamos	we have dinner
centro de la ciudad	city centre
bar(es) de tapas	tapas bar(s)
a pie	on foot
al final de	at the end of

cierra	(it) closes
ino se preocupe!	don't worry!
(muy) tarde	(very) late

¿Qué tal?	This is a handy little question, which can be used to enquire about someone's health, how things are going or how they are getting on with a specific task or activity: the English 'how's it going?' is possibly the broadest equivalent.
Tengo una pregunta	'I have a question'. **Tengo** ('I have') comes from **tener**.
¿Dónde están ...?	'Where are ...?' Adding an 'n' to **está** changes the meaning from 'it is' to the plural 'they are'. We can now contrast **¿dónde está la estación?** ('Where is the station?') with **¿dónde están los bares de tapas?** ('Where are the tapas bars?')
a cinco metros a diez minutos	To say how far away something is (either in distance or in time) we need to use the little word **a** – it equates to the notion of 'away' in English: **Está a diez kilómetros/minutos.** 'It's ten kilometres/minutes (away).'
¿A qué hora es el desayuno? Es a las ocho.	When you're asking at what time something happens, remember to begin the question with **a** ('at').
dígame	Literally 'tell me' – this is used to invite someone to say what they want to say. It's also the usual way to say 'hello' when you answer the phone.
está lejos/cerca	'it's far away/close by'
no se preocupe	'don't worry'. This is quite a complex structure in Spanish, but we can just learn it here as a one-off.

Write out the following numbers in full:

1. 32 ....
2. 44 ....
3. 59 ....
4. 60 ....

5. 67 ....
6. 76 ....
7. 81 ....
8. 93 ....

Can you say the following in Spanish? Check your answers by listening to the audio track. ◉ 31

1. Is it far?
2. It's ten minutes away on foot.
3. The tapas are very good.

• •

Make sure you've understood what is being said in these short dialogues. Listen out in particular for the following information: ◉ 32

1. Where is the hotel, and how many minutes does it take to get there?

. . . .

2. Is the lift on the left or the right, and how many metres away?

. . . .

• •

Look at the map and complete the directions:

• Por favor, ¿dónde está el bar?

• El bar . . . .
  al . . . . de la . . . .
  principal, a la . . . .

• •

The following dialogue has one mistake in each line. Use the language you've learned in this unit to work out what's wrong:

Tourist	Buenos tardes. ¿Dónde está el bar?
Receptionist	La bar está en la calle Salamanca.
Tourist	Muchos gracias. ¿Está lejos?
Receptionist	No, es al final de la calle, a la izquierda.
Tourist	Muy buena. Hasta luego.
Receptionist	Adiós.

Study the following short dialogues based around what time events begin. They're just there for you to read, recognise and use for practice.

1. ¿A qué hora **es** la cena?

    Es a las nueve.

2. ¿A qué hora **cenamos**?

    Cenamos a las ocho.

3. ¿A qué hora **cierran** los bares?

    Cierran a las doce de la noche.

Useful Tips

- notice that the verb in the question is reused in the answer!

- remember the usage of **a** in both the question and the answer.

....

Choose the correct option to complete each sentence:

1. Buenos días. Tenemos una .... reservada.

    a. dormitorio   **b.** hotel   **c.** habitación   **d.** desayuno

2. El restaurante está a .... derecha.

    a. el   **b.** las   **c.** los   **d.** la

3. ¿A qué hora es la cena? Es a las ....

    a. ocho   **b.** una   **c.** mediodía   **d.** tarde

4. ¿Dónde .... el hotel?

    a. es   **b.** está   **c.** hay   **d.** estás

De tapas
Out for some tapas

We'll be looking at the popular Spanish pastime of going out for tapas, as well as learning how to order drinks in a bar.

Traveller's tip

One of the greatest pleasures during your time in Spain will be relaxing over a few leisurely tapas in a bar, taking your time to sample as wide a range as possible.

Until fairly recently, a tapa was a small accompaniment to your glass of beer or wine, served free in some areas of Spain and at a small charge in others. Then suddenly the tapas phenomenon exploded, and various chains of bars geared specifically to tapas sprang up. Many of these have their origins in the Basque Country, where **tapas** - also known as **pinchos** or **pintxos** - are a real art.

Sometimes you'll see a menu; just as frequently, you can take your pick from the tapas on display in a glass case on top of the bar.

You can ask for something as simple as a small tray of olives or peanuts, through croquettes and potato omelette, to fresh squid or any number of elaborately prepared fish- or meat-based titbits. Many come with a portion of bread.

If you'd like more of your favourite tapa, you can order it as **una ración**, served as a larger portion, often in an earthenware dish or on a medium-sized plate.

The joy of tapas - apart from the taste, of course - is that you can have as few or as many as you want, according to your hunger. Equally, you can make the experience last as long as you wish - sitting contentedly in a bar and forgetting about the time suggests you're starting to get into the local routine!

We'll be learning and using several useful new verbs in this unit. These are vital for ordering tapas and drinks.

¿Tiene usted ...?	Do you have ...?
¿Esta tapa tiene ...?	Does this tapa contain ...?
¿Me pone...?	Can I have ...?

 ## Listen up 1

A couple are in a bar, wondering what tapas to order. Their waiter tells them more about the dishes on the menu. Listen to the conversation, but beware: this section may get your mouth watering!

● 33

Words and phrases 1

carta *f* de tapas	tapas menu
a ver	let's see
¿qué es esto?	What's this?
empanada *f*	small savoury-filled pastry
jamón *m*	ham
atún *m*	tuna
cebolla *f*	onion
Es que ...	The thing is ...
vegetariano/a	vegetarian *m/f*
como	I eat
croqueta *f*	meat
carne *f*	croquette
éste *m*/ésta *f*	this (one)
éstos *m*/éstas *f*	these (ones)
queso *m*	cheese

patata *f*	potato
¿me pone ...?	Can I have ...? (lit. will you put (on the bar) for me ...?)
pincho *m* de tortilla *f* de patata	Slice of potato omelette. Also called **tortilla española**, this is made of potato, onion and egg. A plain egg omelette is known as a French omelette (**una tortilla francesa**). You may also know the other meaning of **tortilla** – in Latin America it's a wrap for **fajitas, tacos**, etc.
ahora mismo	right now (coming right up)
chorizo *m* a la sidra *f*	spicy **chorizo** sausage in cider
ración *f*	portion larger than a tapa
pulpo *m* a la gallega	Disks of octopus served Galician-style, with garlic and oil on a wooden platter.
un poco de pan *m*	a bit of bread
¿para beber?	(what can I get you) to drink?
caña *f*	small glass of beer
copa *f* de vino *m* tinto	glass of red wine. **Copa** is used for a 'glass' of wine/spirits; **vaso** for soft drinks. **Tinto** is the word used for 'red' in this context (you can remember it from the English 'tinted'). You can also order **vino blanco** (white) or **rosado** (rosé).
de la casa	house (wine, etc.)
Ahora se lo traigo.	I'll bring it right over.

 ## Unlocking the language 1

¿tiene usted ...?	Have you got ...? **Tiene** is from the verb **tener** ('to have'). We also see **tiene** used to refer to a tapa ('does it have/contain ...?') and the plural **tienen** ('they have/contain ...')
¿me pone ...?	This is from the verb **poner** ('to put') and asks the barman to 'put' the food or drink on the bar. You could also use **¿me da ...?** ('will you give me...?') which we met in Unit 3.

Match the photos of the tapas with their names. You can check your answers online at www.collinslanguage.com/click.

1. pulpo

2. pan

3. croqueta

a.   b.   c.

Find expressions in the dialogue to convey the following: ⊙ 33

1. Have you got a tapas menu?

2. Here you are.

3. It contains tuna and onion.

4. I'm vegetarian (*female*).

5. Can I have two cheese croquettes?

6. Something to drink?

7. Can I have a small glass of beer, please?

Pronunciation Tip

Una **caña**

As we saw earlier, the Spanish **ñ** is pronounced rather like the 'ni' in the English 'onion'. You may have heard it used in common words like **España** (Spain). Try to use it carefully: **caña** is a glass of beer, but **cana** is a grey hair – not something you'd order in a bar!

niño

You may remember 'El Niño' (meaning 'the child') causing chaos a few years ago. Practise the sound in the middle of the word, with a normal 'n' at the start.

Now, using the language you've learned above, think about   ⊙ 34
ordering some different tapas and drinks. How would you say the following? Begin each order with ¿me pone ...? Check your answers by listening to the audio track.

1. three potato croquettes

2. two tuna and onion pastries

3. a portion of bread

4. two small glasses of beer

5. a glass of white wine

Listen to the food and drink orders and make sure you have understood them: 35

1. How many croquettes of each flavour does the first woman order? ....
2. What does the man order with the chorizo? ....
3. Is it two beers and a glass of white wine, or something different for the second lady? ....

. . . .

Have a look back at the Word and phrases 1 and see if you can identify the following tapas from their photos:

1. ....
2. ....
3. ....

a.

b.

c.

. . . .

Match the expressions on the left with their translations on the right:

1. ¿Éstas tienen carne?   with a bit of bread
2. con un poco de pan   three small beers
3. ¿Me pone una tortilla francesa?   Have these got meat in them?
4. tres cañas   Can I have a plain omelette?

 Listen up 2

In the next bar, it's time to order some drinks. You'll hear an order for both hot and cold drinks, as well as some nibbles. 36

¿Qué toman?	What are you having?
café *m* descafeinado	decaffeinated coffee
con leche *f*	With milk. The main coffee orders in Spain are **un café solo** (like an espresso), **un cortado** (as above, but with a small amount of milk) and **un café con leche** (served in a larger cup, with hot milk).
algo para picar	'something to pick at' – Spaniards will often **picar** at appetisers with a quick drink before moving on to a restaurant.
tengo	I have (this is another part of **tener** – to have). We saw it first in Unit 4: **Tengo una pregunta** (I have question).
cacahuete *m*	peanut
aceituna *f*	olive
o	or
patata *f* frita	The term **patatas fritas** (lit. fried potatoes) can be rather confusing, its meaning depending on the context. Here it refers to crunchy crisps but it can also mean French fries.
No puedo comer ...	I can't eat ...

Unlocking the language 2

tomar
: This is a very useful verb, meaning 'to take', in the sense of 'consume'. You can use it to mean either 'eat' or 'drink'.

para picar
: 'to nibble on'. The word **para** features a lot when a waiter is asking you what you want: you might hear **¿para beber?** ('what do you want to drink?'), **¿para picar?** ('do you want some nibbles?') or **¿para comer?** ('do you want to sit down to lunch?')

Find the tapas and drinks hidden in these anagrams:

1. eachacute ....   5. novi ....
2. ñaca ....   6. oracquet ....
3. oppul ....   7. soque ....
4. ozchoir ....   8. facé ....

. . . .

Can you say the following in Spanish? Check your answers by   ⦿ 37
listening to the audio track.

1. Have you got anything to nibble on?
2. Can I have a portion of olives, please?

. . . .

Make sure you've understood what is being said in these short   ⦿ 38
dialogues. Focus on the following:

1. What hot drinks are ordered in the first exchange? ....
2. In the second exchange, is the order for white wine and olives or red wine
   and peanuts? ....

. . . .

Fill in the gaps in this conversation between a barman (camarero) and a
customer (cliente). We've given you some first letters:

Camarero	¿Q..................... toma, señora?
Cliente	Una ración de pulpo, por favor.
Camarero	¿Algo m.....................?
Cliente	Sí, un pincho de tortilla.
Camarero	¿P..................... b.....................?
Cliente	Una caña.

Remember that the main points in this unit have been:

1. asking if someone has something – **¿tiene una carta?**

2. asking if a tapa contains something – **¿tiene carne?**

3. ordering food and drinks – **¿me pone una caña?**

• •

Now see how good your memory is. Can you give the Spanish names for these tapas and this drink?

1. ....

2. ....

3. ....

4. ....

5. ....

6. ....

Choose the correct option to complete each sentence:

1. Buenas tardes. ¿Me da una .... de pulpo?

   a. restaurante   **b.** ración   **c.** chorizo   **d.** pan

2. La empanada no .... carne.

   a. es   **b.** tienen   **c.** está   **d.** tiene

3. .... vegetariano.

   a. Soy   **b.** Estoy   **c.** Tengo   **d.** Tiene

4. ¿Me pone un ...., por favor?

   a. caña   **b.** leche   **c.** cortado   **d.** croqueta

En el restaurante
In the restaurant

6

We'll be focusing on the restaurant experience in Spain, looking at the language you'll need to order what you want, as well as highlighting some of the regional delicacies you might fancy trying.

Traveller's tip

Sitting down to a meal in Spain – whether in a top-class restaurant or a humble set-menu bar – is not an experience to be rushed. Whilst relatively little importance is attached to breakfast, Spaniards have traditionally relished the long lunch or dinner as something to be enjoyed by the whole family. It's interesting to note that both of these meals are eaten far later than you may be used to: lunch in Spain may not begin until 2.00–3.00pm, and dinner can start as late as 9.00–10.00pm and go on until after midnight!

Many visitors' first taste of Spanish food is the legendary **menú del día**, a daily menu offering three multi-choice courses, including certain drinks, for around €10–12.

Higher up the market, restaurants such as El Bulli and Celler de Can Roca, both in Catalonia, have been making waves internationally for the excellence and originality of their cuisine.

If you're eating out, you will notice a range of techniques for diners to attract waiters' attention: whistling, clicking fingers, hissing, etc. These are fascinating to observe, but you wouldn't necessarily want to copy them!

Each region of Spain is fiercely and justifiably proud of its local dishes. In the south, chilled **gazpacho** soup is typical, while the east coast specialises in **paella**. The northern regions of Galicia and the Basque Country are famous for their fish, while in the centre of the country you can enjoy excellent **cocido** stew and a range of meat dishes such as **cochinillo** (roast suckling pig).

With Spain's international reputation for wine production, you can be assured of a fine selection of robust reds, chilled whites, fruity rosés or sparkling **cavas**, all affordably priced, whichever area you're visiting.

¡Que aproveche! Enjoy your meal!

In this unit we'll be sitting down to a three-course lunch and using several useful new structures along the way. We'll learn more about the conventions of ordering food.

¿Qué es …?	What is …?
Hay/¿Hay?	There is, there are/Is there? Are there?
Quiero …	I want …

 Listen up 1

A couple go into a restaurant for a set-menu lunch. Listen to the conversation they have with the waiter, which takes you through the different stages of ordering a meal.

⊙ 39

Words and phrases 1

¿Para comer?	Would you like to sit down to lunch? (lit. in order to eat).
mesa *f*	table
por aquí	this way
de primero	For starters (lit. of the first (course)). Spanish refers, logically, to the first and second courses of the meal, so 'for the main course' is **de segundo**.
hay	there is/there are
gazpacho *m*	Cold soup from Andalucía, made from tomatoes, peppers, cucumber, etc.
ensaladilla *f* rusa	Russian salad (potato and diced vegetables in mayonnaise).
canelones *mpl*	cannelloni

sopa *f*	soup
frío/fría	cold *m/f*
tomate *m*	tomato
pimiento *m*	pepper (vegetable); the variety you shake onto your food is **pimienta** *f*.
quiero	I want
¿para usted?	for you?
para mí	for me
paella	**Paella** is most commonly seafood-based (**de marisco**), but can also involve meat (**de carne**) – often chicken or rabbit – or be **mixta** (seafood and meat mixed) or **vegetal** (vegetable-based).
pollo *m*	chicken
judías *f* verdes	green beans
lomo *m* a la plancha	grilled loin of pork
cerdo *m*	pig, pork
marisco *m*	shellfish
botella *f*	bottle
agua *f* sin gas	still water (lit. water without gas). Sparkling water is **agua con gas** (with gas).

🔓 Unlocking the language 1

hay/¿hay?	'there is'/'there are'. Notice that this one little word serves as both a singular and a plural, as well as the question forms 'Is there ...?' and 'Are there ...?' In this way, Spanish is much simpler than English.
quiero	The verb **querer** means, among other things, 'to want' – here we have **quiero**, 'I want'. Don't worry about sounding too direct in saying that you 'want' something in Spanish.

Find expressions in the dialogue to convey the following. Remember that you can check your answers online at www.collinslanguage.com/click.

 39

1. Have you got a table for two?
2. for starters ...
3. for the main course ...
4. What is gazpacho?
5. I want the Russian salad.
6. Something to drink?
7. two glasses of red wine

Pronunciation Tip

gazpacho

The Spanish 'z' is pronounced a bit like the English 'th', rather than the 'zzz' that might seem logical. There are regional and international variations, but if you aim to say **gath-pat-cho** you won't go far wrong.

Now, using the language you've learned above, think about ordering a range of different starters, main courses and drinks. How would you say the following? Begin each order with para mí ... Check your answers by listening to the audio track.

40

a. chicken with French fries

b. grilled loin of pork

c. chilled soup

d. seafood paella

e. a glass of rosé wine

Listen to these people ordering a meal and write true or false next to 🔘 41
each statement:

1. The first order is for Russian salad and paella. . . . .

2. The second order is for chilled soup and chicken. . . . .

3. The third order is for two beers and a bottle of wine. . . . .

• •

Match the expressions on the left with their 'continuations' on the right:

1.	De primero hay	agua sin gas.
2.	Para beber quiero	para cuatro?
3.	De segundo quiero	sopa o ensaladilla.
4.	¿Tiene una mesa	pollo a la plancha.

 ## Listen up 2

The couple have finished their main courses. Their waiter asks them 🔘 42
what they'd like next. You'll hear that the conversation covers both
desserts and coffees, as well as paying at the end.

Words and phrases 2

¿Qué tal?	General use is 'how's it going?'/ 'how are things?' Here the meaning is 'How was it (the meal)?'
todo	everything
¿Quieren ...?	Do you (*plural*) want ...?
postre *m*	dessert
¿Qué hay?	What is there?
helado *m*	ice cream

flan *m*	**flan** is actually a crème caramel
crema *f* catalana	a dessert very similar to crème brûlée
de chocolate *m*	chocolate-flavoured
de vainilla *f*	vanilla-flavoured – notice the extra letter 'i' in the Spanish word. It's therefore pronounced like the English words 'buy' and 'kneel' plus 'yah'.
de fresa *f*	strawberry-flavoured
cortado	coffee with a little milk
No quiero nada.	I don't want anything.
oiga	(lit. hear!) a polite way of attracting someone's attention
¿Me cobra?	Can I settle up, please? (lit. will you charge me?)
cuenta *f*	the bill/check
tres son de propina	three (euros) are for a tip

🔓 Unlocking the language 2

¿quieren ...?	Another form of the verb **querer** ('to want'). It is used to ask two or more people politely if they want (something): **¿quieren café?** – do you want coffee?
hay/no hay	Notice that the way of making a verb negative is simply to put **no** before it: **hay** – there is; **no hay** – there isn't.
No quiero **nada**.	A stage on from the use of **no**, above, is to sandwich the verb with **no** and **nada**, to produce **no** quiero **nada** – I don't want anything. Don't worry that it might look like an ugly double negative (I don't want nothing) – this is correct and normal in Spanish.
oiga	This is an ideal way of attracting someone's attention politely. It's actually a command form of **oír** (to hear), but nobody will feel ordered about if you say it to them.
tres son de propina	(Lit. 'three (euros) are of tip'). There's no obligation to leave a tip in Spanish bars and restaurants (people often just leave a couple of coins) but there is no harm in leaving 5–10% if you've enjoyed your meal.

¿Me cobra(s)?

Cobrar actually conveys the idea of charging or collecting (money), so you're asking the waiter to charge you. It's the standard – and easiest – way to ask if you can settle up, but you can also say **la cuenta, por favor** – the bill/check, please.

Find the desserts and flavours hidden in these anagrams:

1. ohdeal ....
2. nalf ....
3. refas ....
4. amaceranatalc ....
5. livinala ....

. . . .

Can you say the following in Spanish? Check your answers by listening to the audio track.   ◎ 43

1. I don't want anything.
2. For me, a coffee with a dash of milk.
3. Can I settle up, please?

. . . .

Listen to these short dialogues, and identify which of the options are being asked for: ◎ 44

1. Does the customer ask for:
   a. a coffee and a vanilla ice cream
   b. a crème brûlée and a strawberry ice cream
   c. a chocolate ice cream and some fruit

2. Does the customer ask for:
   a. two black coffees
   b. one white coffee
   c. a coffee with a dash of milk and one white coffee

Each line below has its words in the wrong order. Use the language you've learned above to work out what's wrong:

1. ¿favor cobra por me?

2. tiene cuenta la aquí

3. treinta son señor euros

4. de tres propina son

Let's recap

Remember that the main points in this unit have been:

1. establishing what there is (on a menu) – **¿hay helado de chocolate?**

2. stating preferences/orders – **quiero la paella/quiero un flan/quiero un café**

3. looking at restaurant conventions – **una mesa para dos; de primero/segundo/postre; ¿me cobra?** etc.

• •

Now see how good your memory is. Can you give the Spanish names for these dishes?

1. chilled soup from Andalucía

2. Russian salad

3. chicken with fries

4. grilled loin of pork

5. crème caramel

6. crème brûlée

Choose the correct option to complete each sentence:

1. .... primero hay gazpacho o ensaladilla rusa.
   - **a.** Por
   - **b.** Para
   - **c.** La
   - **d.** De

2. ¿..................... postre?
   - **a.** Son
   - **b.** Quieren
   - **c.** Está
   - **d.** La

3. .... un cortado, por favor.
   - **a.** Son
   - **b.** Para mí
   - **c.** Son
   - **d.** Un

4. Dos euros son de ....
   - **a.** mesa
   - **b.** restaurante
   - **c.** ser
   - **d.** propina

••

Food and drink

It's a good idea to go back through your work and make a list of all the foods and drinks you like, noting any points of cultural interest. Also check over the conventions for ordering, and the things that a waiter/waitress is likely to ask you – in this way you'll be prepared when you make your first trip into a Spanish bar or restaurant!

Repaso 1
Revision 1

Listen up
⊙ 45

Listen to the voicemail left by the manager of a Spanish property company for an English-speaking client, Mr Dobson.

To be doubly sure you've understood, listen to the passage several times with pauses, and try and write down everything the man says. From your notes, answer the following questions:

1. What is the caller's full name? ....
2. Which company does he represent? ....
3. On what street is the house located, and at what number? ....
4. Who has the key – what is her full name? ....
5. At what number is the office located? ....
6. What is her nationality? What language is she said to speak? ....
7. What are her working hours? ....

Speak out
⊙ 46

You might like to think about where you are going for your holidays. How would you say the following in Spanish? Check your answers by listening to the audio track.

1. Are you going to Barcelona?
2. Yes, I'm going to Barcelona.
3. Are you going to Spain?
4. No, I'm not going to Spain.

Or maybe you're going somewhere this afternoon (the museum, the station, class, etc.)? How would you say the following in Spanish?

5. Are you going to the (city) centre?
6. No, I'm going to a restaurant.

Where is ...?

Think about places and items in your life, and where they're located. Perhaps your local bar is at the end of the street on the left, or the railway station is 'near here'. In all these cases of 'location', you'll be using the verb **estar**. Practise asking **¿Dónde está ...?** for places that you go in your area and reply using **Está ...** .

Read the following short text describing a city centre, then answer the questions that follow:

La calle principal está en el centro de la ciudad. Tiene muchos bares y muchas tiendas. Hay cuatro restaurantes en la calle: dos italianos y dos indios. Mi bar favorito es Casa Pepe. Está al final de la calle, a la izquierda. Tiene muy buenas tapas.

1. Where is the main street? ....
2. How many restaurants are there, and what sort of food do they serve?
   ....
3. Where is Casa Pepe located? ....
4. What compliment is paid at the end? ....

At what time?

Look again at the structures for saying at what time things happen (trains departing, etc), as well as the time of day itself. Try to invent a few things relating to a daily timetable: maybe you're going to the museum at two o'clock.

Now try and remember how you would write the following sentences in Spanish:

1. At what time does the train from Madrid arrive? ....
2. It arrives at three o'clock. ....
3. At what time does the bus to Valencia leave? ....
4. It leaves at half past ten. ....

Numbers

Revise the numbers from 0 to 99 carefully. Try to spot and memorise the patterns in clusters (e.g. the teens, twenties) and the rhythm beyond 31.

Now try and say out loud the following Spanish numbers. ⊙ 47
Check your answers by listening to the audio track.

1. 16 ....
2. 20 ....
3. 27 ....
4. 30 ....
5. 31 ....
6. 56 ....
7. 67 ....
8. 78 ....
9. 80 ....
10. 94 ....

Hablando con la gente
Talking to people

7

We'll go deeper into some of the structures we've already covered, to allow you to engage more fully in conversations with people you meet. We'll also learn how to speak to people in a friendlier way.

Traveller's tip

One of the trickiest barriers to overcome when you're learning Spanish and using it to talk to people, is the range of different ways of saying 'you'.

In standard modern English, there is just one form: whether you're talking to one person or ten, to a prime minister or a child, the word is simply 'you'.

In Spanish it's different. So far in this course, we've used what is known as the formal or polite form, generally used when you don't know someone very well and you want to be respectful. This has been characterised by the word **usted** (polite 'you') and a particular verb form to go with it.

In this unit we'll turn our attention to the informal, 'friendly' form, used with someone your age or younger, with whom you feel comfortable and whom you now feel you know a bit better. This is often known as the **tú** form (informal 'you').

With practice you'll know instinctively which form to use. It's safer to start with the polite form so as not to risk offending anyone, but Spaniards will understand that you are not being intentionally rude if you use the wrong form. They will often put you at your ease by saying **trátame de tú** ('speak to me informally') or **nos podemos tutear** ('we can treat each other as **tú**').

In this unit we'll be looking at formal and informal ways of addressing people. We'll also be revising some earlier structures and adapting them.

¿Eres inglés?	Are you English?
¿Vas al centro?	Are you going to the centre?
¿Cuántos años tienes?	How old are you?

 ## Listen up 1

Tom and Linda are on the bus, and bump into Pepe, a man they met the previous day. They're all on their way to do some shopping, but decide to go to a bar for a quick drink first. Listen carefully, as they'll be ordering drinks and also revealing some ages! 48

Words and phrases 1

Nos podemos tutear.	We can call each other (lit. treat each other as) **tú**.
comprar	to buy
unas cosas	some things

tomar algo	to have something to drink
Vamos a este bar	Let's go to this bar
invito yo	It's my treat (lit. I invite). **Invitar** is 'to invite', and is the usual way for someone to say that they're buying the drinks.
pues	well
oye	An informal way of attracting someone's attention (it's also a part of oír – 'to hear' – which we met when we learned the formal **oiga**).
hoy	today
cumpleaños *m*	birthday
felicidades	congratulations
si no es indiscreción	if you don't mind my asking
¿Cuántos años tienes?	How old are you?
Tengo veintitrés años.	I'm 23.
Soy el viejo del grupo.	I'm the old one in the group.
no **te** preocupes	Don't worry (we heard the formal **no se preocupe** in Unit 3).
isalud!	cheers! (lit. health)

 ## Unlocking the language 1

¿Va**s** al centro?
¿Quiere**s** tomar algo?

We're now starting to focus on the informal style of each verb. Generally, this is just the formal 'you' style we've learned (**tiene, quiere, va**) with an –**s** added on (**tienes, quieres, vas**). We'll do plenty more practice, so don't worry if it's a bit confusing at first.

Notice also that **a** + **el** = **al** ('to the')

¿Me pones (me das) tres cañas?

Here's the informal way of asking for drinks. You can now compare it with the formal **¿me pone ...?** or **¿me da ...?**

unos/unas

These are the words for 'some' – one for feminine words and one for masculine words (or a mix of feminine and masculine)

el cumpleaños de Linda	There's no apostrophe in Spanish to allow us to say something like 'Linda's birthday'. Instead, we have to say 'the birthday of Linda'.
¿Cuántos años tienes? Tengo veintitrés años	To ask and give our age in Spanish, we don't talk about being 23, but rather having 23 years. So we use the verb **tener** – **¿cuántos años tienes?** (how many years do you have?); **tengo veintitrés años** (I have 23 years).

↗ Your turn 1

Find expressions in the dialogue to convey the following:　　⊙ 48

1. We can call each other *tú*.
2. Are you going to the centre?
3. Do you want something to drink?
4. It's my treat
5. Congratulations!
6. Don't worry.

Pronunciation Tip

tres cañas

This is a simple point, but often overlooked. Try to pronounce every **s** in Spanish as if it were **ss**, like the end of the word 'hiss' (rather than 'his' – can you feel the difference?). This is easy at the start of a word, but at the end of a word like **tres**, it's easy to slip into a kind of English **z**. Try saying **tres casas** (three houses) like 'tress kass-ass'.

· ·

Speaking informally and using poner, how would you ask for　　⊙ 49
the following? Check your answers by listening to the audio track.

Can I have ...

1. ... three beers, please?
2. ... two glasses of red wine, please?
3. ... a portion of olives, please?

· ·

Listen to the people talking, and focus on the following questions:　　⊙ 50

1. How old is the first speaker? ....

2. The second speaker says 'you are 15' – is the address formal or informal?

....

3. How old is the third speaker? ....

....

Complete the informal column below:

Formal	Informal
¿Cuántos años tiene?	¿Cuántos años tienes?
¿Me da una caña?	....
¿Quiere una patata?	....
¿Va al centro?	....
¿Prefiere ir al museo?	....
¿Dónde está?	....

Listen up 2

Danny chats to Sofía, a Spanish student, in the park. Listen out for details of jobs and studies.

51

Words and phrases 2

perdona	Excuse me – informal command from **perdonar** (to pardon, to excuse).
perdido/a	lost *m/f*
eres	you are (from **ser**)
No eres de aquí	You're not from here
¿verdad?	'are you?' Spaniards often use **¿verdad?** (meaning truth) or simply **¿no?** at the end of statements to turn them into questions, just like we do in English with the tags 'isn't it?', 'can't she?', 'shouldn't I?', etc. The Spanish system is much simpler, as you can see!

estar de vacaciones	To be on holiday. To go on holiday is **ir de vacaciones**.
estudio	I study (from **estudiar**).
academia *f*	language school
hablas	you speak (from **hablar**)
practicar	to practise
guía	Person working as a guide (**guía** is used for both a man and a woman)
trabajo *m*	job/work
trabajar	to work
poco tiempo *m* libre	very little free time
zumo *m* de naranja	orange juice (lit. juice of orange)

 ## Unlocking the language 2

¿estás perdido?
estoy bien
¿estás de vacaciones?

Have a look at the various usages of **estoy** and **estás** in the dialogue, and make sure you have understood why **estar** is used in each case, not **ser**.

On top of these uses, you will also hear **estar** being used to convey temporary feelings and emotions – temporary states of being – to be nervous, happy, excited. Listen out for examples of this.

eres estudiante
no eres de aquí
soy canadiense
soy profesora y guía

Now look at the usages of **ser**, and make sure you are clear as to why it is used in these instances.

eres

This is the informal 'you' form of **ser**. Let's summarise this verb:
soy – I am
eres – you are (informal)
es – you are (polite)

¡Que interesante!

'How interesting!' **Que ...** is a very useful construction for remarking upon something:
¡Que aburrido! 'How boring!'
¡Que bien! 'How lovely!'

me gusta trabajar

The **me gusta** structure works not only with things (**me gusta el estadio/el arte**) but also with activities expressed as verbs: **me gusta trabajar** ('I like working' – lit. 'It pleases me to work')

Here are some anagrams of some informal (ending in -s) Spanish verbs for you to unravel:

1. shabal ....
2. somat ....
3. risquee ....

4. nsete ....
5. sav ....
6. seer ....

• •

Can you say the following in Spanish? Use the informal 'you' where appropriate. You can check your answers by listening to track 52. 52

1. Are you on holiday? ....
2. I'm on holiday. ....
3. I'm fine. ....
4. Don't worry. ....

• •

Listen to the four descriptions (A, B, C and D) and match what is said in each case with the corresponding photo: 53

1. ....

2. ....

3. ....

4. ....

Below are some formal (polite) questions. Use the language you've learned in this unit to change each verb to the informal style:

1. ¿Quiere tomar un café?

2. ¿Tiene mucho tiempo libre?

3. ¿Prefiere ir a un museo o a un restaurante?

4. ¿Va al centro de la ciudad?

Let's recap

In this unit we've looked at the difference between polite and informal ways of addressing people. We've also studied the way to ask and state how old someone is. Here are some model sentences to help you remember:

¿Es (usted) canadiense? (polite)

¿Eres canadiense? (informal)

¿Quiere (usted) ir al bar? (polite)

¿Quieres ir al bar? (informal)

¿Cuántos años tiene (usted)? (polite)

¿Cuántos años tienes? (informal)

Tengo treinta y cuatro años. ('I' – first person singular)

• •

Now see how good your memory is for numbers. Each of the numbers below is misspelt. Try and spot the error, then practise saying the corrected version.

1. 33   trienta y tres

2. 44   cuaranta y cuatro

3. 55   quincuenta y cinco

4. 66   setenta y seis

Choose the correct option to complete each sentence:

1. Tú .... nervioso hoy.

   a. es **b.** eres **c.** está **d.** estás

2. Tú .... 23 años.

   a. es **b.** tienes **c.** eres **d.** tiene

3. Tú .... ir al museo.

   a. tiene **b.** tienes **c.** quiere **d.** quieres

4. Tú .... al museo.

   a. vas **b.** eres **c.** va **d.** está

De compras
Out shopping

8

We'll cover the language you'll need when you go out shopping, and take a look at what sorts of shops you can expect to find.

Traveller's tip

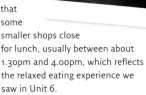

At some point in your trip to Spain, you're bound to fancy a saunter around the shops to see what's on offer and perhaps pick up a bargain.

The first thing you'll notice in Spanish cities is that whilst large chains are of course present, they are less prevalent than would be the case in other European countries. Whereas the UK, for example, is infamous for having branches of the same shops on every high street, Spain's shopping streets offer plenty of traditional, family-run shops and small businesses.

The one department store no city centre is without is **El Corte Inglés**, where you can get pretty much anything. You'll also see foreign stores like IKEA, FNAC, C&A and Habitat, but you'll also be reminded that Spain is the home of international success stories such as **Zara** and **Mango**.

Store opening hours are generally quite long, with most staying open until 8pm, or later in tourist areas. Be aware that some smaller shops close for lunch, usually between about 1.30pm and 4.00pm, which reflects the relaxed eating experience we saw in Unit 6.

Keep an eye out also for local indoor and outdoor markets, selling items ranging from bric-a-brac to fresh fruit and vegetables. If you're on the coast, it's a great experience to wander round a fish market, gaping at the size and variety of what's on offer, and maybe jotting down a few new items of vocabulary.

Whether you're a shopaholic or a retail novice, a dip into the sights, noise and smells of Spanish shopping is always a colourful experience.

In this unit we'll be revising some of the structures we met in earlier units, and will look carefully at the language you'll need to browse and make purchases.

¿Tienen ...?	Have you got ...?
Quiero/prefiero ...	I want/I prefer ...
More numbers	

Listen up 1

Stephanie is looking to buy a shirt for herself. Listen to the dialogues to see how she gets on. Try and pick out the price of the item she buys.

Remember that you can also read all of the dialogues online at www.collinslanguage.com/click.

⊙ 54

Words and phrases 1

¿Qué busca?	What are you looking for? **Buscar** is 'to look for' – you don't need an extra word for 'for'. **Busco** means I'm looking.
camisa *f*	shirt
blanco/blanca	white *m/f*
(de) algodón *m*	(made of) cotton
talla *f*	size (of clothing)
mediano/mediana	medium *m/f*
¿Me la puedo probar?	Can I try it on?
claro que sí	of course
Es un poco pequeña.	It's a bit small (for me).
la dejo	I'll leave it
es un poco cara	it's a bit expensive
otro/otra	(an)other *m/f*. You don't need an additional word for the 'an' in 'another'.

bonito/bonita	pretty *m/f*
Me la llevo.	I'll take it.
Pase por caja, por favor.	Come to the till, please.

Unlocking the language 1

¿Me la puedo probar? Me la llevo.	The various structures with the word **me** are quite complex, so it's best here just to study the two usages and learn the expressions as they appear.
	It is interesting to note, however, that both phrases use **la** because they are talking about **la camisa**. If the item were masculine or plural, it could be **lo**, **los** or **las**.
adjectives	In Words and Phrases we've given you **blanco** and **blanca** for 'white'. Which one you use depends on whether the item being described is masculine or feminine. **Camisa** is feminine, so we say **una camisa blanca**. A white sweater (*masculine*) would be **un jersey blanco**.
this (one)	There's also a masculine/feminine thing going on here. 'This shirt' (*feminine*) is **esta camisa**, but 'this sweater' (*masculine*) would be **este jersey**. If you don't want to repeat the word **camisa** and prefer to say 'this one', you can use **ésta**. You can hear this last variant five lines from the end of the dialogue – the accent is used to clarify the meaning.

Your turn 1

Find expressions in the dialogue to convey the following: ⊙ 54

1. What are you looking for?
2. Here's one.
3. Can I try it on?
4. I'll leave it, thanks.
5. Is it cotton?
6. I'll take it.

Pronunciation Tip

¿Qué quiere?

As is the case in standard English, the **q** in Spanish always comes in the combination **qu**. In fact, you'll only see it as either **que** or **qui**. However, it's pronounced not as the English 'queen' or 'quick', but rather like the *ke* in 'Ken' and the *kee* in 'keep' respectively. Try pronouncing the question **¿Qué hay aquí?** 'What is there here?'

It's time to revise the numbers so that we can state and understand 55
prices. How would you say the following prices? Begin each sentence
with son and end it with euros. Check your answers by listening to
the audio track.

1. 19€ ....
2. 24€ ....
3. 35€ ....
4. 47€ ....
5. 58€ ....

Listen to the people talking and make sure you have understood ⊙ 56
what each person is saying. Then answer the following questions:

1. What problem does the first speaker have? ....
2. Does the second shopper buy the item? ....
3. What does the shop assistant ask the shopper to do? ....

Match the English expressions on the left with their Spanish translations
on the right:

1. I'll take it.   ¿Qué talla busca?
2. What size are you looking for?   Es un poco cara.
3. Can I try it on?   Me la llevo.
4. It's a bit expensive.   ¿Me la puedo probar?

Listen up 2

It's time for more shopping, and there are
some more decisions to be made. Listen
to the conversations; in the first dialogue
the shop assistant is using the polite form
of address, while in the second dialogue,
the customer and the shop assistant are
comfortable using the tú form.

⊙ 57

plato *m*	plate
¿cuál?	which? what?
prefiere(s)/prefiero	you prefer/I prefer
con	with – in prices, **18.50€** is expressed as **dieciocho con cincuenta** (lit. eighteen **with** fifty). Notice that the euro symbol, €, is written after the numbers in Spanish.
vale	okay
¿Se lo envuelvo?	'Shall I wrap that up for you?' You may sometimes be asked **¿Es para regalo?** (Is it a gift for someone?) so that the shop assistant can gift-wrap it beautifully for you at no extra cost.
muy amable	(that's) very kind (of you)
estos/estas	these *m/f*
zapatos *m*	shoes
¿Cómo pagas?	How are you paying?
en efectivo	In cash (you may also hear **en metálico**). Strictly speaking, foreigners in Spain should have their passport ready when using a credit card in a shop.
Marca tu PIN.	Tap in your PIN code (secret number). The formal variant would be **marque su ...**
ya está	that's it – done
¿verdad?	We met this tag word earlier on, where it meant 'are you?' but we said at the time that it can be used to mean a variety of things. Here it means 'aren't they?'
precioso/a/os/as	gorgeous

prefiero/prefiere(s)	We've got used to seeing pairs of verb forms, where the one ending in –o means 'I do' and the other one means 'you do': e.g. **quiero** (I want) and **quiere(s)** (you want). Here's another pair, belonging to the verb **preferir** (to prefer).
Plural adjectives	You'll have noticed that we've said **estos zapatos** for 'these shoes'. Just as 'this' becomes 'these' in English, Spanish has a means of denoting plurals: **este** (this) becomes **estos** (these) and the feminine **esta** (this) becomes **estas** (these).
	Notice also that whereas the **camisa** in the first dialogue was **bonita**, the **zapatos** here are **bonitos**. It all matches up!

↗ Your turn 2

Think about the use of blanco/blanca/blancos/blancas to describe various things as being white. Which is the correct form in each of the cases below?

1. un plato ....
2. una camisa ....
3. cuatro platos ....
4. cinco camisas ....

| 1. | 2. | 3. | 4. |

Can you say the following in Spanish? We're using the polite form. 58
Check your answers by listening to the audio track.

1. Which do you prefer?
2. Shall I wrap it up for you?
3. In cash.

Make sure you've understood what is being said in these short 59
dialogues. Look specifically for the following information:

1. How much is the first item?
2. How will the second shopper pay?

Each line below has its words in the wrong order. Use the language you've learned above to work out what's wrong:

1. su favor por PIN marque ....

2. ¿da pasaporte me su? ....

3. preciosos estos son zapatos ....

 Let's recap

Remember that the main points in this unit have been:

1. stating what you're looking for in a shop – **busco una camisa blanca**

2. wanting and preferring – **quiero esta camisa/prefiero este jersey**

3. work on this/these – **este jersey/esta camisa/estos zapatos/estas camisas**

•••

Now see how good your memory is. Thinking about a shirt (una camisa), how would you say the following?

1. I want a shirt.

2. I want a white shirt.

3. I prefer this shirt.

4. It's pretty.

•••

Choose the correct option to complete each sentence:

1. .... camisas son preciosas.

   a. Este   **b.** Esta   **c.** Estos   **d.** Estas

2. Prefiero .... platos.

   a. este   **b.** esta   **c.** estos   **d.** estas

3. .... jersey es bonito.

   a. Este   **b.** Esta   **c.** Estos   **d.** Estas

4. Quiero .... camisa.

   a. este   **b.** esta   **c.** estos   **d.** estas

Un poco de cultura
A bit of culture

9

We'll take a trip to a Spanish museum, looking at what's on offer, what you can expect to pay, and how to say what you need to say there.

Traveller's tip

Once you've had your initial burst of tapas and shopping, it's time to check out the wealth of historical and contemporary cultural options on offer. Your hotel or the tourist information office will have leaflets telling you where to head for.

In fact, Spanish cities have so much history visible in their streets and buildings that it's not always necessary to visit a museum to get your culture fix. You can plan your day to take in strolls around particular **barrios** (districts/ quarters), where you can not only savour the flavour of an area, but also stop off for a **menú del día** or a few **tapas**.

The larger cities, especially Madrid, Barcelona, Valencia, Sevilla and Bilbao, have a huge range of art galleries (**pinacotecas**) and museums (**museos**) to cover all tastes. Look out for one of various types of city card, giving you discounted entry into certain museums. Having said that, you'll find admission prices are reasonable in Spain, and a good number of buildings are free to enter.

As is the case with shopping, you'll find museum opening times are generous, allowing you to absorb the contents without feeling rushed. If you fancy staying on to have something to eat in the gallery's restaurant – perhaps on a terrace overlooking the city – then so much the better.

ochenta y siete   87

In this unit we'll learn three new structures: saying that we like something, that we're going to do something, and that we want to do something.

Me gusta ...	I like ...
Voy a ir/visitar ...	I'm going to go/visit ...
Quiero ir a ...	I want to go to ...

 Listen up 1

A tourist is at the hotel reception asking for information about a museum. We learn about the museum's location, its opening hours and admission price. See if you can pick these out as you listen.

⊙ 60

❝❞ Words and phrases 1

museo m	museum. **Pinacoteca** means art gallery.
arte m moderno	modern art
si es posible	if possible
claro que es posible	of course it's possible
le	for you
voy a apuntar	I'm going to jot down
direcciones f	directions
papel m	(sheet of) paper
¿Le/Te gusta ...?	Do you like ...?
me gusta (mucho)	I like it (a lot)
a mí también	so do I/me too
entrada f	admission; entry
descuento m	discount
abre	it opens
está abierto	it is open

desde las ocho de la mañana	from 8am
hasta las diez de la noche	until 10pm
ver	to see
muchas cosas	many things
dar una vuelta	to go for a stroll

 ## Unlocking the language 1

Quiero ir/¿Quiere(s) ir?	'I want to go/Do you want to go?' Up to now, we've seen **quiero** used with an item – **quiero un helado** ('I want an ice cream'). You can also use it with another verb to state what you want to do – **quiero ir** ('I want to go').
Voy a ir/visitar	Similarly, you can talk about what you're going to do by using a part of **ir** (e.g. **voy** – I'm going) + **a** + another verb, e.g. **voy a tomar un café** (I'm going to have a coffee), **voy a ir** (I'm going to go).
¿le/te gusta ...? me gusta ...	**Gustar** is often thought of as being the verb 'to like' but it actually means 'to please', so in Spanish, to say you like coffee, you have to turn it round and say that coffee pleases you. That explains the order of **¿Le gusta el arte?** – Does art please you? Similarly, **me gusta el arte** suggests that art is pleasing to me (i.e. I like it). You can add **mucho** for 'very much', or if you don't like something (e.g. coffee), it would be **No me gusta el café**.

 ## Your turn 1

Find expressions in the dialogue to convey the following: 60

1. I want to go to the museum.
2. I'm going to jot down the directions.
3. That's very kind of you.
4. Do you like modern art?
5. Yes, I like it a lot.
6. There's a discount with this card.
7. Now I'm going to go for a stroll.

Pronunciation Tip

hasta luego

Note that the letter **h** in Spanish is used in writing, but is never pronounced. So in the expression **hasta luego** (see you later), the first word is in fact pronounced 'asta'.

Let's have a look at the new structures we've learned in Unlocking the language. How would you say the following plans? There are some hints provided in brackets. Check your answers by listening to the audio track. ⊙ 61

1. I want to go to the art gallery. (*a la pinacoteca*)

2. I'm going to have a glass of wine. (*tomar una copa de vino*)

3. I like art. (*el arte*)

•••

Listen to the people talking, and make sure you have understood what they're saying. Pay particular attention to the following: ⊙ 62

1. What does the first person like and dislike? ....

2. Which building is the second person going to visit? ....

3. What does the third person want to eat? ....

•••

¿Cuándo está abierto? Match the opening times on the left with the corresponding figures on the right:

1. El Guggenheim está abierto desde las nueve hasta las tres.   10.00–8.00

2. El Prado está abierto desde las diez hasta las ocho.   4.00–5.00

3. El Camp Nou está abierto desde las siete hasta las doce.   9.00–3.00

4. El Alcázar está abierto desde las cuatro hasta las cinco.   7.00–12.00

During his visit to a museum, Mike buys his entry ticket, gets some
assistance from a guide and later strikes up a conversation with
another visitor. Listen to the dialogues.

⊙ 63

Words and phrases 2

adulto *m*	adult
entonces	so/therefore
un veinte por ciento	20% – notice that you have to include **un** – literally '**a** 20%'.
contemporáneo/a	contemporary
sección *f*	section
grande	big
en la sala *f* principal	in the main hall
folleto *m*	leaflet
escultura *f*	sculpture
experto/a	expert *m/f*
exposición *f*	exhibition
comentario *m*	Commentary – it can also mean simply 'comment'.
resto *m*	rest (remainder)
quedamos	**Quedar** here means 'to rendezvous'. So here, Carmen is saying 'shall we meet at 3.00?'
hasta las tres	See you at 3.00 (lit. until 3.00)

vamos/quedamos

These are verb forms indicating that 'we' are doing the action. Let's take a moment to summarise the various 'persons' of some of the main verbs we've met:

	I	you (polite)	we
ser	soy	es	somos
estar	estoy	está	estamos
tener	tengo	tiene	tenemos
ir	voy	va	vamos
querer	quiero	quiere	queremos
preferir	prefiero	prefiere	preferimos

 Your turn 2

Use the words below to fill the gaps in the sentences below. It's an informal dialogue:

hoy   Es   Hay   quieres   quedamos   gusta

.... una exposición de arte .... en el museo. .... muy interesante. ¿Te .... el arte? Si .... ir, ... a las once.

• •

Can you say the following in Spanish? Check your answers by listening to the audio track.   ⊙ 64

1. I prefer sculpture.
2. I'm not an expert.
3. Shall we meet here at two o'clock?

Make sure you've understood what is being said in these short dialogues.

Dialogue 1:

1. How much is it to get in?

2. What discount is offered with the card?

Dialogue 2:

3. Until what time is the building open?

. . . .

Each line below has its words in the wrong order. Use the language you've learned above to work out what's wrong:

1. al ir contemporáneo quiero de museo arte ....

2. escultura no pero soy gusta me la experto ....

3. una hay dos las a exposición ....

⟳ Let's recap

In this unit we've looked at what we want to do, what we are going to do, and what we like. Here are some model sentences to help you remember:

(no) me gusta (mucho) el arte moderno

(no) quiero ir al museo

Voy a visitar una galería.

. . . .

Choose the correct option to complete each sentence:

1. Tiene un .... por ciento de descuento.

   a. grande   **b.** diez   **c.** este   **d.** no

2. El museo no .... abierto hoy.

   a. soy   **b.** estoy   **c.** es   **d.** está

3. ¿Cuánto .... la entrada?

   a. soy   **b.** euros   **c.** es   **d.** son

4. Quiero .... muchas cosas.

   a. estar   **b.** ver   **c.** museo   **d.** ir

Vamos al fútbol
Off to the football

10

We'll look at the language you'll need to buy a ticket for a Spanish football match, as well as learning something about the country's biggest sporting rivalry!

Traveller's tip

Any fixture between Barcelona and Real Madrid is not just a football match – it's a geographical and political battle between two historical rivals. Real Madrid, based in the capital, was favoured by General Franco, whose four decades of brutal dictatorship to 1975 repressed and alienated regions with separatist tendencies, such as Catalonia and the Basque Country. Catalan football fans have long memories, and the passion whipped up every time Barça plays Real is something to behold.

Equally feisty – and for similar reasons – is any game between Athletic de Bilbao and either of the big Madrid teams. Athletic was formed at the end of the 19th century by a combination of Basque students returning home from the UK, and migrant workers from the North-East of England working in the Basque Country's shipyards and steelworks. The English link explains the name 'Athletic', and the team's red-and-white-striped shirts are a cultural borrowing from Sunderland FC.

You'll struggle to get a ticket for many of the biggest encounters, but on less extreme occasions it's relatively easy to get a ticket to see a first division match. You can check out a club's website for details of fixtures and prices, or visit the ground a day or so before the game.

The default kick-off time is 5.00pm on a Sunday, but TV obligations mean that there are usually a couple of games on a Saturday night (sometimes starting as late as 10.00pm) and later into Sunday evening. Check in the press or ask at the tourist information office.

Inside the ground, you'll notice that trouble is extremely rare, and that there is some chanting but far less 'singing' than you might be used to. Be prepared to join the rest of the crowd in a cry of **goooool** when the home team scores!

In this unit we'll be revising some of the structures we've learned in earlier units, including directions, prices and times. We'll also look at a couple of twists on existing verbs, and will be learning some useful exclamations.

¿Para ir al estadio de fútbol?	How do I get to the football stadium?
Tiene que ...	You have to ...
¿A qué hora es el partido?	What time is the match?
El delantero es muy bueno.	The striker is very good.

Listen up 1

Tom is a real footy fan back home, so he wants to see a match during his holiday in Spain. He asks a passer-by for directions to the football stadium. Listen out for a mode of transport and a distance in metres. ◉ 66

Tom buys some tickets for the match at the stadium ticket office. Can you pick out the price, and the time the match kicks off? ◉ 67

Outside the stadium, Tom asks a scarf-seller for directions. They are both young, so they speak to each other informally using tú. ◉ 68

Words and phrases 1

estadio *m* de fútbol *m*	football stadium
tiene que	you (*polite*) have to
coger	to take/catch (public transport)
partido *m*	match
entrada *f*	ticket (for entry to an event – see also museums in Unit 9).
clase *f*	type/class
general	general – here referring to a basic class of ticket in the cheapest section of the ground.
Gol Sur	(behind the) south goal – geographical points are a common way of denoting an area of the ground.

si tiene	if you've got (any)
en total	in total
bufanda *f*	scarf
dame	give me – an informal command form, but it's courteous and normal, nonetheless.

 ## Unlocking the language 2

Tiene que coger …	'You have to catch …' We've seen plenty of usages of **tiene**, but this is a new one. When a part of **tener** is followed immediately by **que**, the meaning shifts to obligation: not 'to have', but 'to have to' (do something).
hasta	**Hasta** can mean 'until' with reference to time or 'as far as' with reference to location. You saw it in Unit 9 in the context of time: **Está abierto hasta las diez de la noche** 'It's open until 10pm.' Here, however it takes the other meaning: **Tiene que coger el metro hasta Avenida del Estadio** 'You have to take the metro as far as Avenida del Estadio.'
Es a las cinco.	To say that something 'is' (in the sense of 'takes place' or 'happens') at a particular time, we use the verb **ser** – hence **el partido es a las cinco.**
dame	This is an informal command form of **dar** ('to give'). Don't worry about ordering people to do things in this way – it's completely normal in Spanish. You can always add **por favor** if you feel squeamish.

Find expressions in the dialogues to convey the following: ⊙ 66-68

1. To get to the football stadium, please?
2. What time is the game?
3. I want two tickets, please.
4. That's 32 euros in total.
5. Here on the left, 50 metres away.
6. Give me two.

Pronunciation Tip

general/coger

The letter **g** in Spanish is complicated, with its various pronunciations depending on the letters around it. Many of these are guessable, but the two to watch out for are **ge** and **gi**. For each of these, you have to produce a guttural sound a bit like the 'ch' in the Scottish 'loch'. Try saying **general** (general) and **gitano** (gypsy). If you find it impossible, you can get by with a heavy English 'h' – 'hen-er-al'.

Note that the same sound has to be applied to every instance of the letter **j**. Examples include words like **mejicano** (Mexican), **jefe** (boss) and the boy's name **Javier**.

Look at the three sentences below, then find their Spanish equivalents in the dialogue. Try to memorise the Spanish expressions, then say them out loud: ⊙ 69

1. How do I get to the football stadium?
2. What time is the match?
3. I want two tickets, please.

Listen to the people talking, and make sure you have understood what they're saying.

⊙ 70

1. When is the match taking place? ....
2. How many tickets are bought? ....
3. Which means of public transport is recommended to get to the stadium?

....

¿Dónde está? Write out these directions in English. The map below may help you.

1. (A) Está al final de la calle. ....
2. (B) Está a la izquierda, a ochenta metros. ....
3. (C) Está cerca de aquí. ....
4. (D) Está aquí a la derecha. ....

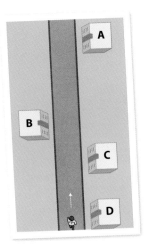

Inside the stadium just before the game, Tom and Rachel chat to the 71 man in the next seat. His name is Manolo and he's a bit older than they are, so they use the polite form. You'll hear some comments as they go through the game, and a quick summing-up at the end.

Words and phrases 2

¿Qué le parece ...?	What do you think of ...?
maravilloso/a	fantastic *m/f*
ustedes	you (plural of **usted**)
equipo *m*	team
mejor	better
vamos a ver	let's see
qué pasa	what happens
fuera de juego	offside
árbitro *m*	referee
nervioso/a	nervous *m/f*
gol *m*	goal
no se preocupe	don't worry
normalmente	normally
marcan	they score
¡qué bien!	great!
¡ojalá!	if only!
córner *m*	corner-kick
delantero *m*	striker
vago/a	lazy *m/f*
en fin	anyway/at the end of the day
punto *m*	point
Hasta otro partido	See you at another game sometime

Unlocking the language 2

¿Qué le parece ...? What do you think of ...? A great way of asking someone their opinion on what follows – in this case **el estadio** (the stadium).

ustedes Simply the plural form of **usted** – Manolo is addressing both Tom and Linda, so rather than **usted es**, he says **ustedes son**.

estoy nervioso	Remember from earlier that if you want to describe how you're feeling (a temporary state or condition e.g. angry, tired, bored), you'd say **estoy** – e.g. **estoy nervioso**
es vago	The striker is referred to as lazy using **es vago**, as it's deemed to be a characteristic – as opposed to the temporary state/condition we described above.
el minuto noventa	It's 'the minute 90' rather than 'the 90th minute'.
¡ojalá!	A great little expression which is flexible enough to mean 'if only', 'let's hope so', 'chance would be a fine thing' and more. It comes from the Arabic *Inshallah* – 'God willing'.

↗ Your turn 2

Here are some anagrams of Spanish words associated with a football match for you to unravel:

1. tiadrop ....

2. antdare ....

3. budafan ....

4. rátibor ....

5. log ....

Can you say the following in Spanish? Check your answers by listening to the audio track.   ⊙ 72

1. I want to see a goal.

2. offside

3. We've got a corner.

4. goal!

Make sure you've understood what is being said in the expressions you'll hear: ⊙ 73

1. Which player in the team is mentioned by his number, and what is the speaker's opinion of him? ....

2. Does the speaker like the stadium? ....

3. How many points have we won in the match? ....

4. What is the meaning of the fourth speaker's farewell? ....

Each line below has its words in the wrong order. Use the language you've learned in this unit to work out what's wrong:

1. ¿el parece le estadio qué? ....
2. poco un delantero el vago es ....
3. bufandas favor por dos dame ....

⟳ Let's recap

In this unit we've looked at what we 'have to do', and the difference between what we 'are' characteristically (ser), versus temporary or geographical factors (estar). Here are some model sentences to help you remember:

Tiene que coger el metro.

Soy escocés, soy de Edimburgo, soy artista, soy viejo, soy inteligente.

Estoy nervioso, estoy en el estadio.

• •

Now see how good your memory is. Each of the sentences below has one error. Try and spot it, then practise saying the corrected version.

1. Quiero ir a la estadio
2. El partido está a las cinco.
3. El delantero es muy buena.
4. Dame dos entrada, por favor.
5. Me gusto mucho el equipo.

Choose the correct option to complete each sentence:

1. El estadio .... maravilloso.

    a. está   **b.** son   **c.** están   **d.** es

2. .... un poco nervioso hoy.

    a. Soy   **b.** Estoy   **c.** Somos   **d.** Son

3. ¿A qué hora .... el partido?

    a. está   **b.** donde   **c.** es   **d.** son

4. ¿Dónde .... el estadio?

    a. es   **b.** metro   **c.** ser   **d.** está

La vida nocturna
Nightlife

11

We'll consider some options for extending your days in Spain into the night. Having had tapas in Unit 5 and a meal in Unit 6, we'll now be paying a visit to a lounge bar for a nightcap and a bit of live jazz.

Traveller's tip

We've all heard stories of revellers coming back from Ibiza or Benidorm and boasting about how late they were able to stay out drinking. In fact, away from the tourist areas, the purpose of Spain's relatively relaxed licensing laws is to allow people to unwind gently, unhurriedly, having taken in a good meal beforehand. Eating and drinking generally go hand in hand, and can make the evening far more enjoyable than just a binge.

Having been open since breakfast time, normal bars in cities will generally (and understandably!) start to shut down between 11.00pm and midnight. After this, many Spaniards will head for what is known as **un pub** - a term borrowed from the English (though pronounced closer to 'paff') and used to denote what we might call a lounge bar. Pubs will generally close after 1.00am - sometimes as late as 3.00 or 4.00am - and will allow you to relax with a drink in comfortable surroundings, often listening to live or recorded music.

You also have the option of a nightclub - **una discoteca**. The tourist information office or your guidebook will give details of styles of music and DJs favoured by specific clubs.

It's worth noting that Spain's public smoking policy requires pubs and bars to declare themselves smoking or non-smoking and stick to it. You'll see stickers on the door or window, or above the bar, saying **En este bar se puede fumar** (smoking allowed) or **En este bar no se puede fumar** (forbidden). Some have designated areas devoted to each preference.

In this unit we'll be learning the language of making suggestions, and also looking at ways of saying what events are happening.

¿Vamos a un pub? Shall we go to a lounge bar?
¿Por qué no tomamos algo? Why don't we have a drink?
Esta noche toca un grupo. There's a band playing tonight.

 Listen up 1

Katie and Ben are with their new friend Eduardo, and they're wondering what to do after dinner. See if you can pick out where they head for.

◉ 74

A little later on, they're lucky enough to find a bar with live music.

◉ 75

🔊 Words and phrases 1

¿Qué quieres hacer ahora?	What do you want to do now?
no sé	I don't know
Podemos tomar una copa.	We could (lit. we can) have a drink.
¿Conoces algún sitio?	Do you know a (lit. any) place?
¿Por qué no vamos?	Why don't we go?
Hay muchos bares y pubs allí.	There are lots of bars and pubs there.
¡Qué bien!	Great!
esta noche *f*	tonight
toca un grupo	a group is playing
¿entramos?	shall we go in?
jazz *m*	jazz. Departing from the usual pronunciation of the Spanish **j** and **z**, this foreign word is pronounced like it is English, but with more of a 'y' sound at the beginning.

¡genial!	great! fantastic! cool!
mesa *f*	table
barra *f*	bar/counter
ginebra *f* con tónica *f*	gin and tonic. You will also hear **un gin-tonic**
con mucho hielo *m*	with a lot of ice
le podemos pedir ...	we can order ... for him
una copa de cava	A glass of cava (sparkling wine from Catalonia, in the north-east of Spain).
buena idea	good idea

Unlocking the language 1

Podemos ...	'We can/could ...'
¿Por qué no ...?	'Why don't we ...?' These are both standard ways in Spanish of making suggestions. **Podemos** comes from the verb **poder** ('to be able', incorporating ideas of 'can', 'could', etc.) It's used for 'can' in terms of permission (**podemos entrar** – we're allowed to go in) and in many contexts of possibility/ability (**podemos ir al museo** – 'we can/could go to the museum').
¿Conoces algún sitio?	'Do you know a place?' **Conocer** is used for 'to know' when we mean being acquainted with a person or a place. **Saber** is used when we are referring to knowledge of a subject.
Toca un grupo.	'There's a band playing.' Notice that in Spanish the word order can differ greatly from the English equivalent, so here we're actually saying: 'Plays a band'. Don't worry about this: you'll be understood whichever order you use!

Find expressions in the dialogue to convey the following: ⊙ 74–75

1. What do you want to do now?

2. We could have a drink.

3. Do you know a place?

4. There's a band playing.

5. Shall we go into this pub?

6. We're going to the bar.

. . . .

Match the names of the drinks with the photos:

1. una copa de cava

2. una ginebra con tónica

3. una caña

a.   b.   c.

Pronunciation Tip

barra

The Spanish **rr** generally needs a lot of work to be mastered. It's often said that Scots have an advantage here, as their trilled 'rrrr' is what is required. Practise rolling your **rr** with as many vibrations as you can manage, then try pairs of words with **r** and **rr**: e.g. **para** ('for', which we've met) and **parra** (which means 'grapevine'). The ultimate nasty is **prórroga** ('extra time', in football), which has one of each! For extra practice, you could try this tongue-twister: **El perro de San Roque no tiene rabia.** (St Roch's dog hasn't got rabies.)

How would you say the following? Check your answers by
listening to the audio track. 76

1. What do you want to drink? *(use the informal form)*

2. a glass of cava

3. with a lot of ice

· ·

Listen to the people talking, and make sure you have understood
what they're saying. Here are some questions to guide you: 77

1. What does the first person want with his gin and tonic? ....

2. What drink does the second person order? ....

3. What is happening tonight, and at what time? ....

· ·

Making suggestions. Match the suggestions on the left with the activities
on the right:

1. ¿Por qué no ...   tomar algo, Ana?

2. Podemos ...   entramos en este bar?

3. ¿Quieres ...   a un pub?

4. ¿Vamos ...   ir al museo si quieres.

 Listen up 2

Later the same evening, Katie, Ben and Eduardo are having fun
in the jazz bar. Listen out for more drinks, the possibility of a dance,
and arrangements for getting back to the hotel. 78

cantante	Singer – **cantante** is both masculine and feminine, but we can hear that a female singer is referred to here – **la cantante**.
canta	He/she sings – from **cantar**, 'to sing'.
guapo/a	good-looking
tío/tía	Literally 'uncle' and 'aunt', these two words are used colloquially in a way equating to the English 'mate' or 'man', as in 'Come on, mate!' – **¡venga, tío!**
¿Por qué no pido más bebidas?	Why don't I order more drinks? **Pido** is from **pedir** ('to order').
¿Os apetece algo más?	Do you fancy something else (to drink)?
bailar	to dance
no importa	it doesn't matter
hombre	Literally the word for 'man', **hombre** can be used to speak directly to someone in expressions like **¡venga, hombre!** (come off it, man!). The person being addressed needn't be a man!
¡venga!	come on!
tengo calor *m* tengo sueño *m*	I'm hot I'm sleepy
baño *m*	toilet – you may see or hear various terms for the restrooms in public buildings: **baños, aseos, servicios, WC.**
chico/chica	boy/girl
estoy cansado/a	I'm tired *m/f* – this is used more for bodily weariness; **tengo sueño** (see above) refers to feeling sleepy.
¿Llamamos un taxi?	Shall we call a taxi?
volver	to return/go back
buenas noches	good night

¿Os apetece ...? 'Do you fancy ...?' This is another back-to-front structure, very like the work we did on **me gusta**. **Apetecer** is like the English 'to appetise', so we're really saying 'Does another drink appetise you (or appeal to you)?' The new element here is the **os** – its function is the same as **te** ('you') we met earlier, but this time it refers to more than one person. The net result is: 'Does it appetise you (people)?'

tengo calor/sueño 'I'm hot/sleepy.' A number of expressions that would start with 'I am' in English begin with **tengo** ('I have') in Spanish. Here we're actually saying 'I have heat' rather than 'I'm hot'. Here's a short list of similar expressions:

tengo calor – I'm hot
tengo frío – I'm cold
tengo hambre – I'm hungry
tengo sed – I'm thirsty
tengo sueño – I'm sleepy
tengo suerte – I'm lucky

Llamamos un taxi/¿Llamamos un taxi? 'Let's call a taxi/Shall we call a taxi?' It's reassuring to see that there's absolutely no spelling change involved in turning a statement into a question – just add the question marks!

↗ Your turn 2

Here are some anagrams of several words and expressions used in the dialogue. Can you solve them?

1. relongcoat ....
2. neatcant ....
3. arbila ....
4. sabbied ....
5. codansa ....

••

Can you say the following in Spanish? Check your answers by listening to the audio track. (◎) 79

1. I don't dance very well.
2. I'm going to the toilet.
3. I'm sleepy.
4. Shall we call a taxi?

Make sure you've understood what is being said. Answer the ◉ 80 following questions as you listen to the people talking:

1. What is said about the group's singer? …………………………………
2. What solution is suggested to relieve the heat? …………………………………
3. How far away is the hotel? …………………………………
4. When will they next see each other? …………………………………

....

Look at the questions on the left and fill in the answers on the right. This may seem a bit repetitive, but you're practising changing the endings of the verb forms. The first row has been completed to start you off.

1. ¿**Quieres** una caña?   Sí, **quiero** una caña.

2. ¿**Bailas** bien?   Sí, ……………… bien.

3. ¿**Tienes** calor?   Sí, ……………… calor.

4. ¿**Estás** cansado?   Sí, ……………… cansado.

5. ¿**Vas** a la barra?   Sí, ……………… a la barra.

🔄 Let's recap

In this unit we've looked at various ways of making suggestions. Here are some model sentences to help you remember:

¿Vamos a un pub?

¿Por qué no vamos a un pub?

Podemos ir a un pub.

¿Quieres ir a un pub?

We also learned some useful new expressions with tener.

Now see how good your memory is. Below are some English expressions – give the Spanish for each, but in the negative form:

e.g. I'm sleepy   **no** tengo sueño

1. I'm from Madrid. ....
2. I want a glass of cava. ....
3. I'm thirty years old. ....
4. I'm going to the WC. ....

• •

Choose the correct option to complete each sentence:

1. .... ir a tomar algo.

   a. Vamos   **b.** Podemos   **c.** Tú   **d.** Estoy

2. ¿Por .... no pedimos más bebidas?

   a. tengo   **b.** qué   **c.** para   **d.** caña

3. Esta noche .... un grupo.

   a. jazz   **b.** estás   **c.** doce   **d.** toca

4. .... a llamar un taxi.

   a. Tú   **b.** Hay   **c.** Vamos   **d.** Tienes

Mantenerse en contacto
Keeping in touch

We'll consolidate what we've learned so far in the course, as well as looking ahead to meeting up with our new Spanish friends in the future.
To do this, we'll be having a look at the language of communication – phones, mobiles, texting and email.

Traveller's tip

It's great to make friends in Spain during your visit, and to keep in touch once you're back in your own country. It's an ideal way to practise the language, as well as giving you a social foundation for future visits.

These days, your mobile phone – **el móvil** – and email – **el correo electrónico** – are the two most common tools for keeping in touch. In fact, you may already have used email in Spain – in **un cibercafé** (internet café) – and may be used to phoning or texting home by mobile.

You'll see that Spaniards are every bit as technologically savvy as foreign visitors and that there are a range of telephony companies working in tandem with your mobile service provider back home. Don't be surprised if, when you switch on your cell phone on emerging from the airport in Spain, your screen lights up with the name of a local telephone network.

Roaming rates have dropped spectacularly over the last couple of years, but if you want to contact friends and family living in Spain while you're there on holiday, you also have the option of buying a Spanish SIM card or even a cheap Spanish mobile.

Cibercafés can be found in most Spanish towns and cities, and rates tend to be very reasonable. You may even find your hotel has internet facilities available to guests.

In this unit we'll be revising questions and answers in the context of making plans for the future, using the language of communication.

¿Me mandas un correo electrónico?	Will you send me an email?
Te mando un SMS.	I'll send you a text.
¿Cuál es tu número de teléfono?	What's your phone number?

We'll also have a look at the two tricky words **por** and **para**.

Katie and Ben have reached the end of their holiday, and are swapping contact details with their new friend Eduardo. Listen out for two phone numbers and an email address.

⊙ 81

The trio have a farewell drink together before Katie and Ben leave for the airport. You'll hear departure and arrival times for the flight, and a decision on how to get to the airport.

⊙ 82

¡Llámame!
(00 34) 686 315061
Fernandez.maria@
hotmail.com

Remember to access the written dialogues online if you think that it will help you remember.

Words and phrases 1

¿Cuál es tu número de teléfono?	What's your phone number?
te lo apunto	I'll jot it down for you.
necesitas	You need (from **necesitar** – to need).
el prefijo de la provincia	The regional code (lit. the prefix of the province).
mi número *m* de móvil *m*	my mobile number
te doy	I'll give you (from **dar** – to give)
mi dirección *f* de correo *m* electrónico	my email address

la penúltima	one (drink) for the road (lit. the last-but-one)
patatas bravas	A *tapa* consisting of chunks of fried potato with a spicy tomato sauce.
en seguida	right away
avión *m*	aeroplane
os acompaño al aeropuerto	I'll come with you (lit. I'll accompany you) to the airport.
coger un taxi	to get a taxi
es más barato	it's cheaper (lit. it's more cheap)
de todas formas	anyway

 # Unlocking the language 1

¿Cuál es tu número de teléfono?

'What (lit. which) is your phone number?' Notice the word order – your number of telephone.

Es el tres, cuarenta y ocho, cero seis, noventa y uno.

'It's 3480691.' The style of giving phone numbers in Spanish takes a bit of getting used to. Firstly, 'it's' is **es el**. Digits are stated in pairs – forty-eight, ninety-one, etc. If there's an odd number of digits, the first one is said on its own, then the pairs begin. A pair beginning with zero (e.g. 06) is pronounced **cero seis** ('zero six'). These conventions take a bit of getting used to, so listen to the dialogue again and focus on how the numbers are given.

el prefijo

'the code'. To ring Spain from abroad you'll need the international code from your own country, then 34 (**treinta y cuatro**) for Spain, followed by the province-specific code – this is 91 (**noventa y uno**) for Madrid, 93 (**noventa y tres**) for Barcelona, and so on. Then you continue with the person's number.

el correo electrónico

'electronic mail'. Increasingly, Spaniards are using the English 'email' or the jocular **emilio** (based on the Spanish male name).

ben.thompson44@ myemail.co.uk

The convention for pronouncing an email address is: **ben-punto-thompson-cuarenta-y-cuatro-arroba-myemail-punto-co-punto-u-k**
The key words here are **punto** for 'dot' and **arroba**, meaning 'at'. If there's no dot and you want to say 'all one word', use **todo junto**.

os acompaño

'I'll accompany you'. The **os** is something we saw during Unit 11 – remember it means 'you' and refers to two or more people (in this case, Ben and Katie). For clarity, compare the following, both spoken by Eduardo:

Te acompaño, Katie
Os acompaño, Katie y Ben

🔺 Your turn 1

Find expressions in the dialogue to convey the following. Remember that you can check your answers online at www.collinslanguage.com/click.   81-82

1. What's your phone number?
2. I'll jot it down for you.
3. Have you got a mobile?
4. I'll give you my email address.
5. I'll come with you to the airport.
6. We can take a taxi.

Pronunciation Tip

número, penúltima

We've seen a lot of words in this course with a written accent, and we've talked earlier on about why the accents are there. Don't worry just yet about writing these – but remember that the important thing when you're speaking is to emphasise the syllable on which the accent is written. Say the words out loud: **nú-me-ro; pen-úl-ti-ma.**

How would you say the following? Two answers are given to get you started. Check your answers by listening to the audio track. 83

Mi número de teléfono es el ...

1. 456702 – cuarenta y cinco, sesenta y siete, cero dos
2. 8456702 – ocho, cuarenta y cinco, sesenta y siete, cero dos
3. 550794
4. 2713601
5. 3162982

Two Spanish friends are giving you their email addresses, but you haven't picked up some of the letters. Try and write down the missing letters as you hear them:

Te doy mi dirección de correo electrónico:

1. ol _ pe _ _.se_ _ll_ @ y _ h_ _.e _
2. n _ r_ a.l _ p _ _ @con _ _ c _ _ _ e._ _ _

· ·

Match the questions or suggestions on the left with the English translations on the right:

1. ¿Me das ...?	Have you got ...?
2. ¿Tienes ...?	What's ...?
3. ¿Cuál es ...?	We could ...
4. ¿Me apuntas ...?	Will you give me ...?
5. Podemos ...	Will you jot down for me ...?

 ## Listen up 2

Katie and Ben have reached the airport. Now it's time to say goodbye to Eduardo. Listen out for more contact details, as well as various ways of saying goodbye.

¿Me mandas un SMS (un mensaje corto)?	Will you send me a text? The word **texto** for 'text message' isn't official in Spanish yet, so you still tend to hear either **SMS** or **mensaje corto** (short message). **Mandar** is 'to send'.
desde Londres	from London
por supuesto	of course
ya lo tengo	I've got it now
las fotos	the photos – notice that it is spelt with an **f**– rather than a **ph**–
¡Qué desastre!	What a disaster!
dame dos besos	Give me two kisses – the standard greeting or farewell gesture (one kiss on each cheek).
gracias por todo	thanks for everything
hasta otra visita	See you on the next visit (lit. until another visit)
¡cuídate!	look after yourself/take care
hasta el año que viene	see you next year (lit. until the year that comes).
hasta pronto	see you soon (lit. until soon).
buen viaje	safe journey/have a good trip

Unlocking the language 2

Tenemos que coger	We have to catch – remember that when a part of **tener** is followed by **que**, it means 'must' or 'have to'.
¿Me mandas ...? Te mando ...	Notice that Spanish can imply an action in the future even when the speaker is using the simple present tense. What the Spanish is literally saying is 'You send me ...?'/'I send you ...'. But in English a future tense works best: 'Will you send me ...?'/'I'll send you ...'

Por *or* para?	Both of these words can mean 'for' so they can cause confusion for students of Spanish. There isn't space here to go into detail, but as a simple rule, use **para** when you're talking about the purpose, intended use or destination of something (**el tren para Madrid**) and **por** if you mean 'because of', 'on account of', etc. (**gracias por todo**).
Hasta ...	We learned earlier that this means 'until' (and, for location 'as far as'). This is very useful when you want to say 'see you (at some point in the future)': **hasta mañana** (see you tomorrow), **hasta pronto** (see you soon), **hasta el año que viene** (see you next year).

Your turn 2

Can you remember the expressions needed to construct this short dialogue in Spanish? Refer to the dialogue above if you need to: ⊙ 85

1. Have you got my email address? ....
2. Yes, I've got it. ....
3. I'll send you the photos tomorrow. ....
4. Thanks for everything. ....
5. See you soon. ....
6. Have a good trip. ....

• •

Can you say the following in Spanish? They're all fragments of language to do with communication. Check your answers by listening to the audio track. ⊙ 86

1. I haven't got a mobile
2. It's (*when introducing your phone number*)
3. the area code
4. dot (*in an email address*)
5. at (*in an email address*)

Listen to one person giving an email address, and another giving a phone number. Try and write them both down as you listen:

1. ....
2. ....

Write out these phone numbers in full. The first answer is given to get you started:

1. 8231697   ocho/veintitrés/dieciséis/noventa y siete
2. 7247642   ....
3. 9183240   ....
4. 5670306   ....
5. 3418299   ....

🔄 Let's recap

In this unit we've looked at various structures to do with exchanging contact information. Here are some model sentences:

Mi número de teléfono es el cuatro, veintidós, sesenta y siete, cero ocho. (4226708)
Mi dirección de correo electrónico es: ana-punto-gomez-arroba-hispanichat-punto-com (ana.gomez@hispanichat.com)

Now see how good your memory is. Can you remember how to say:

1. Have you got my address?
2. I've got your number.
3. Two ways of saying 'I'll send you a text'.

Choose the correct option to complete each sentence:

1. Gracias .... todo.

   a. de   **b.** para   **c.** por   **d.** en

2. Hasta el .... que viene.

   a. mañana   **b.** año   **c.** visita   **d.** hora

3. Os .... a visitar.

   a. quiero   **b.** prefiero   **c.** tengo   **d.** voy

4. ¡ .... viaje!

   a. Bueno   **b.** Buena   **c.** Buen   **d.** Buenos

Repaso 2
Revision 2

Age

Remember that in Spanish we 'have' an age, rather than 'being' it. Make sure you can say your age using **tengo ... años**.

Listen up 1

 88

Listen to the people talking about their ages, and write down how old each person is:

1. Raquel ....
2. Pablo ....
3. Marta ....
4. Fernando ....

tú and usted

Your use of the informal and polite versions of Spanish verbs will depend very much on what sort of people you're mixing with, and the formality of the situations you experience. It's a good idea to take some time out and listen again to all the dialogues we've covered, practising converting polite verbs to informal, and vice versa. Remember that in most cases, the informal variant will have an **–s** on the end (e.g. **quieres** – versus the polite **quiere**).

For a bit of practice, try changing the following polite forms into informal versions. The first one is done for you:

Polite	Informal
1. ¿Quiere una caña?	¿Quieres una caña?
2. ¿Es usted canadiense?	....
3. ¿Va usted a Madrid?	....
4. ¿Tiene sueño?	....
5. ¿Habla español?	....

Want to/have to/am going to

Have a look over these structures, and set up a stock of things you can talk about that you want to do (**quiero visitar el Museo Guggenheim**), have to do (**tengo que estudiar**) and are going to do (**voy a tomar un café**).

If you're into culture and leisure activities and want to learn more about what Spain has to offer in your field of interest, the internet is a great source of information. You can start by doing a search for your favourite activity/sport, including key words like 'Spain' in the search. Many official and informal Spanish websites have little flags where you can click to read the information in a number of languages: why not click the English text to read what you want to know, then try reading the Spanish version to see how much you understand. You can print off key pages and look at the two versions side by side, using a dictionary to highlight useful vocabulary. It's a great way of building up your vocabulary and your confidence in areas of interest. If you like sport, you can try searching terms like '**federación española de** (+ *name of sport taken from dictionary*)' to access a wealth of information. Similarly, if you like theatre, cinema, ballet, museums, etc., you can take key words from the dictionary and type them into a search engine. Once you get bitten by the Spanish bug, there will be no stopping you!

Shopping

You've seen that there are a lot of conventions in the language of shopping. Have a look back through the dialogues, and try substituting the items bought for items you'd be likely to buy in Spain. Make a vocabulary list to increase your confidence.

Speak out

⊙ 89

Can you remember how you'd say the following? Try saying the sentences out loud. Check your answers by listening to the audio track.

1. I'm looking for a white shirt.

2. How much is it?

3. It's a bit small.

4. I'll take it, thanks.

Likes and dislikes

Starting with the simple formula of **me gusta …** or **no me gusta …**, you can very easily cover your likes and dislikes. Remember that you don't have to limit this to items or concepts (**me gusta el café, me gusta el arte**); you can talk about activities too (**me gusta estudiar**). Asking others about their preferences is easy, too: there's the informal **¿te gusta…?** or the polite **¿le gusta…?**

By adding **mucho** (or even **muchísimo**) to **me gusta**, you can tell people that you like something 'a lot', while by adding **nada** to **no me gusta** you can express a heartfelt dislike for something: **me gusta muchísimo el té pero no me gusta nada el café.**

Listen up 2

Listen to the people talking about their likes and dislikes, and answer the questions below:

1. Sonia likes sparkling wine – true or false? ....

2. What does Javier like? ....

3. Paco likes Madrid very much – true or false? ....

4. To what extent does Marisol like working? ....

Out and about

If your interests coincide with some of the scenarios we've set up on this course – museums, eating out, a football match, shopping – then you've got a good linguistic platform on which to build. But don't forget that all the structures will be transferable to other situations, and with a bit of dictionary work to get hold of the specific vocabulary for your preferred activity, you'll be able to work out what you want to say.

Communication

Write down all of your contact details, then think about pronouncing everything in Spanish. It's a good idea to write it all out 'longhand' – e.g. if your phone number begins 348 then write down '**tres, cuarenta y ocho**'. This is especially important for your email address: remember the magic words **punto** for 'dot' and **arroba** for '@'. Keep practising these until you find you can say them all fluently without referring to your paper, and don't forget the expressions for texting.

¡Mucha suerte!

Good luck!

HAVE YOU SEEN OUR FULL SPANISH RANGE? PICK A TITLE TO FIT YOUR LEARNING STYLE.

Collins Easy Learning Series

The bestselling language resources, perfect if you're learning Spanish for the first time or brushing up on rusty language skills.

Dictionary
£8.99

Grammar
£6.99

Verbs
£6.99

Words
£6.99

Complete 3-in-1 volume
£10.99

Conversation
£6.99

Idioms
£5.99

Collins Easy Learning Audio Courses

This exciting course allows learners to absorb the basics at home or on the move, without the need for thick textbooks or complex grammar.

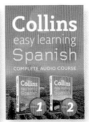

Audio Course stage 1
£9.99

Audio Course stage 2
£12.99

Complete Audio Course (1 and 2) £17.99

Collins products are available from all good bookshops nationwide.
For further information visit: www.collinslanguage.com

Collins